Chicago Manual of Style (CMS): The Easy Way!

Peggy M. Houghton, Ph.D.
Timothy J. Houghton, Ph.D.

Editor: Michele M. Pratt

Education is one of the best investments you will ever make…and our books maximize that investment!
Houghton & Houghton

Baker College
Flint, MI

ISBN: 978-0-923568-89-4

For more information, contact:

Baker College Bookstore
bookstore@baker.edu
800-339-9879

LIBRARY OF CONGRESS CATALOGING-IN-PUBLICATION DATA

Houghton, Peggy M.
  Chicago manual of style (CMS) : the easy way! / Peggy
M. Houghton, Timothy J. Houghton.
      p. cm.
  Includes bibliographical references and index.
  ISBN 978-0-923568-89-4 (alk. paper)
  1. Chicago manual of style--Handbooks, manuals, etc. 2.
Printing--Style manuals. 3. Authorship--Style manuals. I.
Houghton, Timothy J., 1961- II. Title.

  Z253.H73 2008
  808'.0270973--dc22

                                        2008025879

Manufactured in the United States of America

Table of Contents

Preface

After more than thirty years of teaching experience, the authors of this handbook have learned that there has been considerable confusion with writing according to *The Chicago Manual of Style* (CMS) guidelines. Those who are familiar with CMS format realize that many students are apprehensive and rather perplexed with this particular writing style.

Although CMS writing style is designed for those who intend to publish, numerous colleges and universities adhere to these stringent guidelines. Years of experience have proven that there are consistent questions and misunderstandings regarding the style. Consequently, this document has been developed to simplify the CMS writing experience. There are some CMS points that are optional; therefore, the instructor should be consulted for final authority with regard to writing assignments.

The intent of this handbook is simply to supplement *The Chicago Manual of Style* (15th edition). It is provided as a condensed version of the actual manual. Due to the official manual's length, not all topics of the writing style are covered in this book. It is not intended to supersede the manual, but rather reduce its complexity. This explains the title: *Chicago Manual of Style (CMS): The Easy Way!*

The handbook is divided into four parts. Part one focuses on the mechanics of CMS format; part two explains grammar and punctuation usage; part three emphasizes source citation (notes and bibliographies system and author-date system); and part four provides a sample paper.

Note: Some names given throughout the handbook are fictitious.

Part One
Mechanics of CMS

Utilizing Microsoft Word

(for applications prior to Microsoft Word 2007)

The following are specific instructions on how to set up a CMS document using Microsoft Word.

Margins

All margins (top, bottom, and sides) should be set at one inch. Microsoft Word allows the user to set the margin at a default of one inch. To do so, follow the guidelines below:

Margins

1. Under FILE, select PAGE SETUP.

2. Select MARGINS tab and type 1" at TOP, BOTTOM, LEFT, and RIGHT boxes. Click OK.

Alignment/Line Spacing

All documents following CMS guidelines are required to be aligned left and double-spaced throughout the entire document. Be sure not to include additional spacing between paragraphs, sections, etc. To set the default, follow these guidelines:

Alignment/ Line Spacing

1. Place the cursor at the start of the document; select FORMAT.

2. Under FORMAT, select PARAGRAPH.

3. Under PARAGRAPH, set ALIGNMENT to LEFT.

4. Under PARAGRAPH, set LINE SPACING to DOUBLE. Click OK.

Font Type and Size

The entire document should be developed using the same font type and size. The actual font type and font size in CMS should be an easily readable font such as 12-point Times New Roman or 12-point Courier. However, do NOT use Sans Serif

Font Type and Size

fonts, as these do not clearly distinguish between 1, l, and I. To set both the font size and style using Word, do the following:

1. Under FORMAT, select FONT.

2. Under FONT, select Times New Roman or Courier.

3. Under SIZE, select 12. Click OK.

> This is an example of 12-point Times New Roman.
> `This is an example of 12-point Courier.`

Paragraph Indentation

All papers typed in CMS format require paragraphs to be indented one-half inch. This can easily be accomplished by striking the TAB key on the keyboard.

To set the tab to the one-half inch default, do the following:

1. Under FORMAT, select PARAGRAPH.

2. Under PARAGRAPH, select TABS.

3. Under TABS, set DEFAULT TAB STOPS at .5". Click OK.

Hanging Indents

To set the hanging indent feature, do the following:

1. Under FORMAT, select PARAGRAPH.

2. Under SPECIAL, choose HANGING. Click OK.

Page Numbering

Page numbers are placed in the upper right-hand corner of the document. Page numbering should begin with page two (2) on the first page *after* the title page. The title page does not contain a page number.

Page numbering should appear one-half inch down from the top margin. Additionally, the page header is right justified. This can be accomplished using the HEADER AND FOOTER function:

1. Under VIEW, select HEADER AND FOOTER.

2. Select the page number icon (the first icon on the left with

the # symbol); the number will appear on the left side of the box.

3. Highlight the number.
4. Click the align right key located in the toolbar.
5. Click CLOSE.
6. Under INSERT, select PAGE NUMBERS. Uncheck SHOW PAGE NUMBER ON FIRST PAGE. Click CLOSE.

Utilizing Microsoft Word 2007

The following are specific instructions on how to set up a CMS document using Microsoft Word 2007.

Margins

1. Select PAGE LAYOUT from the ribbon tabs.
2. Select the MARGINS icon from the PAGE SETUP drop down menu.
3. Select CUSTOM MARGINS. Type 1" for the TOP, RIGHT, LEFT, and BOTTOM margins. Before leaving this setup, select APPLY TO: Whole Document, then click OK.

Alignment/Line Spacing

1. Select HOME from the ribbon tabs.
2. Select the PARAGRAPH tab window, and choose LINE SPACING by selecting the LINE SPACING icon.
3. Select LINE SPACING OPTIONS, and select ALIGN-MENT LEFT.
4. Select LINE SPACING to DOUBLE, and click OK.

Font Type and Size

1. Select HOME from the ribbon tabs.
2. Select the FONT window.
3. Select either Times New Roman or Courier.
4. Select SIZE of 12.

Paragraph Indentation

1. Select HOME from the ribbon tabs.

2. In the PARAGRAPH window, select LINE SPACING and LINE SPACING OPTIONS.

3. At the bottom of the pop-up window, select TABS. Default TAB STOPS at .5", and click OK.

Hanging Indents

1. Select HOME from the ribbon tabs.

2. In the PARAGRAPH window, select LINE SPACING and LINE SPACING OPTIONS.

3. Under SPECIAL, choose HANGING; click OK.

Page Numbering

Page numbers are placed in the upper right-hand corner of the document. Page numbering should begin with page two (2) on the first page *after* the title page. The title page does not contain a page number.

Page numbering should appear one-half inch down from the top margin and is right justified. This can be accomplished by the following:

1. Select INSERT from the ribbon tabs.

2. Click PAGE NUMBERS in the HEADER/FOOTER box.

3. Select the PAGE LAYOUT ribbon tab.

4. Click PAGE SETUP; click LAYOUT tab.

5. Under HEADER/FOOTER, check the box next to DIF-FERENT FIRST PAGE. Click OK.

Part Two
Grammar and Punctuation Usage

Personal Names

Capitalization. Both real and fictitious names of individuals are capitalized. Except when initials are used alone, the space between the initials should be the same as the space between the last initial and the name.

Robert S. Tower	S. K. Schafer	JFK

Hyphenated and extended names. Hyphenated last names or names that consist of two or more elements should include the name(s) in its entirety.

Martin Luther King	Deborah Dimas-Curtis

Titles and Offices

Capitalization. In general, when civil, military, religious, and professional titles precede a personal name, they are capitalized. However, when these titles follow a name or are used in place of a name, they are lowercased.

President Reagan; the president

Provost Swanson; the provost

Reverend Anthony M. Tocco; the pastor

Pope Benedict XVI; the pope

David M. Wolshon, professor of marketing

Other academic designations. Student status and names of degree are lowercased.

sophomore	master's degree	doctorate degree

Terms of respect. The title itself is capitalized. Articles such as *the* that precede the formal name are lowercased.

the First Lady	Your Honor

Ethnic, Socioeconomic, and Other Groups

Capitalization. Capitalize the names of national and ethnic groups.

African Americans; African American culture
Caucasians; Caucasian culture

Class. Lowercase lettering is used when denoting socioeconomic classes.

the upper class; upper class classification
the elite; elite classification

Names of Organizations

Capitalization. Full names of legislative, administrative, and judicial bodies are capitalized. Articles such as *the* that precede the formal name are lowercased.

the United States Senate; the upper house of Congress
the Federal Bureau of Investigation; the FBI
the United States Supreme Court; the Supreme Court

Institutions and companies. Full name of institutions and companies (and their respective departments) are capitalized. Articles *(the)* that precede the formal name are lowercased.

the Detroit Symphony Orchestra; the orchestra
the Kmart Corporation; the corporation

Associations and conferences. The full name of associations and conferences are capitalized. Articles such as *the* that precede the formal name are lowercased.

the League of Women Voters; the league
Leadership: Impact, Culture, and Sustainability 2008; the conference

Historical and Cultural Terms

Historical events. Major historical events are capitalized. However, historical events known by their generic descriptions are lowercased. Articles such as *the* that precede the formal name are lowercased.

Histori-
cal and
Cultural
Terms

> the Industrial Revolution

Sporting events. Full names of major sporting events should be capitalized. Articles such as *the* that precede the formal name are lowercased.

> the MLB World Series

Academic subjects, course of study, and lecture series. Unless part of an official course name, academic disciplines are not capitalized. Official course names are capitalized. Names of lecture series are capitalized. Likewise, individual lectures are capitalized and generally enclosed in quotation marks.

> A course in 21st century leadership has been developed.
>
> Enrollment begins January 1 for Leadership in the 21st Century.
>
> The last lecture, "CEOs Granting Apologies," was exceptionally interesting.

Calendar and Time Designations

Calendar
and Time
Designa-
tions

Days of the week, months, and seasons. Days and months are capitalized; seasons are lowercased.

> Friday   winter   the spring equinox

Holidays. Secular and religious holidays, specially designated days, and specially designated seasons are capitalized.

> Christmas Day   Lent   New Year's Day

Time and time zones. Time and time zones are lowercased when spelled out (except for proper nouns). Abbreviations are capitalized.

eastern standard time; EST	daylight saving time

Military Terms

Armies and battalions. Armies, battalions, and similar titles are capitalized. Unofficial, yet well-known names, are capitalized as well. When used independently or not as part of the official title, words such as *army* and *navy* are lowercased.

United States Army	National Guard
Union army (American Civil War)	

Wars and revolutions. Major wars and revolutions are capitalized. When using generic terms, lowercased lettering is used.

Gulf War	Korean War; the war

Books and Periodicals

"The" in periodical titles. When *the* precedes newspaper and periodical titles in text, even if *the* is part of the official title, it is lowercased.

She reads the *Washington Post* daily while riding on the bus.

Words to italicize. Official names of periodicals should be italicized.

Many college and university students subscribe to *Fortune* magazine.

Words not to italicize. When the names of newspapers or periodicals are part of the name of a building, organization, prize, etc., they are not italicized.

Los Angeles Times Book Award	Tribune Tower

Poems and Plays

Titles of poems. Quoted titles of poems are usually set in roman type and placed in quotation marks. Poetic work that is exceptionally long, however, is italicized and not placed in quotation marks.

> Chaucer's *Canterbury Tales*

First lines. Poems that are referred to by a first line, as opposed to title, are capitalized in sentence format (according to the capitalization used in the actual poem).

> "To Mr. Paul Gaimard"

Titles of plays. Quoted titles of plays are italicized.

> Wilde's *The Importance of Being Earnest*

Unpublished Works

Written works. Unpublished works such as theses, dissertations, copies of speeches, etc., are placed in roman type, capitalized as titles, and placed in quotation marks. No quotation marks are used with the names of manuscript collections. Titles of soon-to-be published books that are under contract may be italicized, but state *forthcoming* or *in press* in parentheses following the title.

> Correspondence and other material can be found in the Ronald Reagan Collection at the library at the University of Texas.
>
> Houghton & Houghton's *Writing at the College Level* (forthcoming) is due out in September.

Movies, Television, and Radio

What to italicize. Movie titles, television programs, and radio programs are italicized. A television series single episode is set in roman and placed in quotation marks.

> Chevy Chase played a phenomenal role in *Caddyshack.*

Electronic Sources

Analogy to print. Periodicals or complete works are italicized if information is available on the Internet or in CD-ROM format (even if the information exists in print format). Additionally, articles or sections of works are placed in roman and, when required, placed in quotation marks.

> The most recent issue of the *Journal of Leadership and Organizational Studies* is now available.

Online sources. Book titles are italicized. Articles, poems, short stories, etc., are set in roman and enclosed in quotation marks.

> Copies of Cohen's *A Class With Drucker: The Lost Lessons of the World's Greatest Management Teacher* are available in the bookstore.
>
> "Business Etiquette" is the most read article in the journal.

Web sites. If web sites are titled, they should be set in roman, headline style, without quotation marks.

Electronic files. File names may be italicized or set in roman. Additionally, they may be capitalized or lowercased.

> Under **My Documents**, double click the file *classroom management*.

Musical Works

Operas and songs. Titles of operas and songs are italicized. Titles of songs are set in roman, capitalized exactly like poems, and placed in quotation marks.

> *Carmen* is one of the best operas I have ever seen.

Recordings. Album and CD names are italicized. The performer or ensemble is set in roman. Individual song titles are set in roman and placed in quotation marks. Capitalization copies that of poems.

> James Taylor performed "Something in the Way She Moves" on his *Greatest Hits* CD.

Paintings, Graphic Art, and Sculpture

Paintings and statues. Titles of paintings, statues, and other works of art are italicized. The names of works whose creators are generally unknown are set in roman. Photograph titles are set in roman and placed in quotation marks.

> Vincent van Gogh's painting *Starry Night* has quite a history.

Cartoons. Titles of well known cartoons or comic strips are italicized.

> | *Mutts* | *Doonesbury* | *Beetle Bailey* |
> |---------|--------------|-----------------|

Exhibitions. Exhibition and fair titles are not italicized. Catalog titles are italicized.

> Our Body: The Universe Within was recently exhibited at the Detroit Science Center

Numbers

General rule. In general, the following are spelled out: whole numbers from one through one hundred, round numbers, and any number beginning a sentence. Numerals are used for other numbers.

> Our academic institution is over two hundred years old.
>
> The university plans to add 35 employees within the next several years.
>
> Eighteen people were in the building at the time of the fire.

Round numbers. Whether used exactly or as approximations, round numbers such as hundreds, thousands, hundred thousands, and millions are spelled out (except in the sciences).

> Approximately three hundred million people watched the Superbowl game.

Numbering beginning a sentence. Numbers that begin a sentence are spelled out.

> Two hundred and six people were reported injured after the tornado struck a small town in Mississippi.

Consistency and flexibility. Consistency should be maintained where many numbers occur within a paragraph or a series of paragraphs. If numerals are used based on the given rule, use numerals for all in that category. However, in the same sentence or paragraph, items in one category may be listed as numerals and items in another spelled out.

Numbers

> The student population grew from 95 in 2001 to 797 in 2007.
>
> Several buildings caught fire–one of 116 stories and two of more than 30–and some were totally demolished.

Ordinals. Follow the general rule of consistency.

> Ben scored two goals in the third period.

Large numbers. Both numerals and spelled-out numbers are used to express extremely large numbers.

> The dinosaur was believed to be 2.5 million years old.
>
> The U.S. deficit is three trillion dollars.

Physical Quantities

Simple fractions. Simple fractions are spelled out.

> The recipe called for three-quarters of a cup of sugar.

Physical Quantities

Whole numbers plus fractions. Quantities that consist of both a whole number and a fraction may be spelled out when short in length. However, sometimes it is better to express the number and fraction in numerals.

> Sally ran three and three-quarter miles.
>
> Katie required 5 ¾ skeins of yarn to complete the afghan.

Abbreviations and symbols. When using an abbreviation for a unit of measure, the quantity is expressed as a numeral.

> The car averaged 45 mph during the expressway road trip.

Percentages

Percentages. Percentages are given in numerals.

> Out of all of the candidates, 55 percent qualified for the position.

Divisions in Publications and other Documents

Books. Numbers that refer to pages, chapters, parts, volumes, etc. are set as numerals. Likewise, numbers referring to illustrations or tables are set as numerals. Front matter pages are generally in lowercase roman numerals; those for the remaining part of the book are in arabic numerals.

> The preface of the book can be found on pages vi–x; chapter one covers pages 1–16.

Periodicals. References to volumes, issues, and pages of a journal are listed in this sequence with arabic numerals. The words *volume* and *page* are not included.

> My professor's article was published in the *Journal of Leadership and Organizational Studies* 27, no. 2 (2007): 21–37.

Dates

The year alone. Unless a year begins a sentence, it is expressed in numerals.

> The 2004 presidential election created great skepticism.
>
> Twenty twenty-four will be a presidential election year.

The day of the month. Cardinal numbers are used when expressing dates. When a day without a month is listed, the number is spelled out.

> February 6, 2008, was a cold and snowy day.
>
> We will only practice on the sixteenth this month.

Centuries. Centuries are spelled out and lowercased.

> The nineteenth century

Time of Day

Spelled-out forms. Even, half, and quarter hours of time are spelled out in text. When using *o'clock*, the number is always spelled out.

> The meeting will resume at one thirty.
>
> Tomorrow I need to get up at four o'clock.

Numerals. When citing exact times, numerals are used (with zeros for even hours). If using a.m. or p.m., use lowercase lettering with a period following each letter (do not space after the period).

> She plans to make connections on the 10:20 bus.
>
> The plane to Chicago leaves at 6:10 a.m. and arrives at 8:20 a.m.

Noon and midnight. Do not use numerals to express noon or midnight.

> The meeting was adjourned at noon so that the participants could have lunch.

Names

Titles of works. To designate the sequel to a novel or movie, roman numerals are utilized.

> *Star Trek II*

Military and judicial divisions. Ordinal numbers of one hundred or less relating to political or judicial divisions are spelled out.

Military units.

> Second infantry division

Judicial divisions.

Tenth Precinct	Twelfth District Court

Places of worship. Ordinal numbers that are part of the official name of worship are spelled out.

First United Methodist Church

Plurals and Punctuation of Numbers

Plurals. Numbers in their plural form are spelled out. Numerals form their plurals by adding *s* (no apostrophe is required).

Traditional students generally graduate from college in their twenties.
The Rolling Stones were in their prime in the 1970s and 1980s.

Comma between digits. Commas are used between groups of three digits, counting from the right, in numerals of one thousand or more. However, no commas are used in page numbers, addresses, and years.

4,612	49,856	56,139,065
The college is located at 1116 West Bristol Road.		

Inclusive Numbers

When to use the en dash (–). The en dash is used between two numbers that imply *up to and including* or *through.*

The test will cover pages 79–159.

When not to use the en dash. The en dash should not be used if the word *from* or *between* is placed before the first of two numbers. Instead, *from* should be followed by *to* or *through* and *between* should be followed by *and.*

from 1995 to 1997	from March through June
between 110 and 120	

Quotations

Run in or set off explained. Quotations can be either run in – integrated into the text in the same type size as the text and placed in quotation marks – or set off from the text as block

Quotations

quotations. Block quotations are not placed in quotation marks and begin with a new line.

In general, length determines whether to use the run in or block. A short quotation is run in. One hundred words or more – or at least eight lines – are set off as a block quotation.

Initial Capital or Lowercase Letter

Capital to lowercase initial letter: run-in quotations. A quotation that is used as a phrase in a sentence begins with a lowercase letter. Capitalize the first word in a direct quotation. Do not capitalize the first word of a direct quotation when it is blended into the main sentence.

> The doctor suggested, "Take two aspirins and call me in the morning."
>
> The golf foursome always adhered to the "forward is good" philosophy.

Capital to lowercase letter: block quotations. The beginning letter of block quotations can be lowercased based on the syntax of the quote.

**Quotations:
Initial
Capital or
Lowercase
Letter**

> Robbins and Judge (2007) note that although coworkers don't necessarily have legitimate power, they can have influence and use it to sexually harass peers. He further states that
>> although coworkers appear to engage in somewhat less severe forms of harassment than do supervisors, coworkers are the most frequent perpetrators of sexual harassment in organizations. How do coworkers exercise power? Most often it's by providing or withholding information, cooperation, and support. (p. 480)

Introductory Phrases and Punctuation

Use of the colon. Formal introductory phrases are followed by a colon.

> There are two critical things team leaders never do: they do not blame or allow specific individuals to fail, and they never excuse shortfalls in team performance.

Use of the comma. A comma is used after verbs such as *said*, *asked*, etc.

> Dr. Ruiz said, "I will not prescribe any medication for this type of disease."

Paragraphing

Paragraph indention. Block quotations should reflect the original paragraphing.

Text following a block quotation. If the wording following a block quotation is a continuation of the paragraph that introduced the actual quotation, it begins flush left. If, however, the text following the block quotation starts a new paragraph, a paragraph indentation is necessary.

Poetry

Setting off poetry. Block quotations are used for two or more lines of verse. If independent, a poetry quotation is generally centered on the page.

Long lines and runovers. Lines that are too long to appear as a single line are indented one em from the line above.

> They had seen enough strange sights to know how seldom
>   they are real.

Quotation Marks

Quotations and "quotes within quotes." Quoted words, phrases, or sentences are placed in double quotation marks. When using quotations within quotations, use single quotation marks.

> Dr. Finley stated, "This is 'top notch' work."

Placement of closing quotation marks. Periods, question marks, and exclamation points are placed within the set of quotation marks when the actual quotation is a complete sentence.

> Dr. Connie Harrison stated, "It's all in how you choose to look at it!"

Ellipses

The three dot method explained. Most general and many scholarly works use the three-dot method. No more than three spaced periods are used, regardless of where the omission occurs.

> Questions that define an academic institution's culture include many . . . how do outsiders describe the institution? . . . do politics exist within the institution? . . . what is the hierarchy of command?

Paragraphs or beginnings of paragraphs omitted. When one or more paragraphs within a quotation are omitted, three ellipsis points should be placed at the end of the paragraph preceding the omitted portion. However, if the portion omitted is the first section of the paragraph, the paragraph should be indented and three ellipsis points used before the first quoted word.

> . . . Each of the more than 3,000 colleges and universities has a distinct mission.

The three-or-four dot method explained. Poetry and most scholarly works use the three-or-four dot method. Three dots imply that one or more words were omitted within the sentence. Four dots indicate that one or more sentences were omitted.

If using three dots, a space occurs both before and after each period. When using four dots, however, the first dot is the actual period. As such, there is no space before the first period.

> Achieving diversity . . . does not require quotas.
>
> People are comfortable knowing that a college education is imperative. . . . A bad situation would be if that education was not financially viable.

The three-or-four dot method with other punctuation. A comma, a colon, a semicolon, a question mark, or an exclamation point may be placed before or after three ellipsis points. However, they are never used within four ellipsis points.

> As a result, . . . schools have experienced declines in minority populations.

Deliberately incomplete sentence. Three dots are placed at the end of an intentionally grammatically incomplete sentence.

> Most people know that the "Star Spangled Banner" begins "Oh, say, can you see, by the dawn's early light..." But how many individuals know the entire lyrics?

Whole or partial paragraphs omitted. Omitting one or more paragraphs within a quotation is indicated by four ellipsis marks at the end of the paragraph prior to the omitted portion. However, if the paragraph ends with an incomplete sentence, only three ellipsis marks are required.

When the first part of a paragraph is omitted within a quotation, a paragraph indention and three ellipsis marks are placed before the first quoted word.

> A college education now has the status that a high school education had a decade or so ago. . . . The public now sees that education helps boost the economy.

Ellipsis points in poetry. Omitting a portion of the end of a line of poetry is indicated by four ellipsis marks (if what precedes the marks is a complete sentence) or by three ellipsis marks (if what precedes the marks is an incomplete sentence).

> The night quickly grew dark. . . .
>
> Spinning like a windmill . . .

Citing Sources in Text

Full source given. A source in its entirety can be given in parentheses immediately following a quotation. Or, part of the data may be inserted into the text, with specific details placed in parentheses.

> (Robert K. Yin, *Case Study Research: Design and Methods* [Thousand Oaks: SAGE Publications, 2003], 83).
>
> As stated in Yin's *Case Study Research: Design and Methods* (SAGE Publications, 2003), the design of a study is extremely important.

Ibid. The term *ibid* (set in roman) may be used in place of other bibliographic information in a second parenthetical reference if the passage is from the same source and is cited closely to the first. This is only allowed if there are no intervening citations from other sources. It should be followed by a period, a comma, and the page number of the source (if necessary).

> (ibid., 231)

Sources Following Run-in Quotations

No period preceding source. Cite the source after the closing quotation mark of a run-in quotation, and follow with the remaining words or punctuation of the sentence.

> Dr. Williams noted, "College attendance can increase financial standing" (*Leadership*, 281).

Question mark or exclamation point. A quotation placed at the end of a sentence that is itself a question or exclamation requires the punctuation to come *before* the closing quotation mark. The final period is added *after* closing the parentheses.

> "Why would you think that?" (ibid., 285).

Sources Following Block Quotations

Placement and punctuation. The source of a block quotation is typed in the same font size and is placed in parentheses at the end of the quotation. The first parenthesis is typed after the final punctuation mark of the quotation. There are no periods either before or after the final parenthesis.

> (Robert K. Yin, Case Study Research: Design and Methods [Thousand Oaks: SAGE Publications, 2003], 83)

Poetry. Poetry citations are placed on the line below the final line of the quotation. The citation can be centered on the last letter of the longest line of the quotations or set flush right.

> My glass shall not persuade me I am old,
>
> So long as youth and thou are of one date;
>
> But when in thee times furrows I behold,
>
> The look I death my dates should expiate.
>
> (Shakespeare, "Sonnet 22")

Illustrations

Placement and Numbering

Placement. Illustrations should appear as soon as possible after the initial text reference in printed works. They may, however, be placed after the reference if they appear on the same page or same two-page spread as the reference or if the text does not allow appropriate space to list all figures and tables after their respective references.

When illustrations are dispersed throughout the entire document, it must be indicated in the manuscript approximately where each is to be located (use *see 6.8*) (in roman).

Text references and numbering. If several illustrations are utilized in printed works (or in online work), numbers should be utilized and all text references related to them should be as numbers.

| as indicated in figure 6 | refer to figures 6 and 7 |

Illustrations: Placement and Numbering

Continuous versus separate numbering. Illustrations are numbered in one continuous sequence throughout a document. However, if more convenient, maps may be numbered separately. In works that are published in both print and electronic format, illustrations that appear exclusively in the print version or the electronic version must be numbered separately so that the numbering throughout each version is logical and sequential.

Numerals and letters. Use arabic numerals for all illustrations. When a figure consists of several parts, letters may be utilized.

| fig. 11 | fig. 11.2b |

Illustrations in a gallery. Unless referred to in the actual text, illustrations that are gathered in a gallery do not need to be numbered.

Captions

Illustrations: Captions

Syntax, punctuation, and capitalization. A caption may consist of a few words, an incomplete sentence, a complete sentence, several sentences, or a combination. If a caption is an incomplete sentence, no punctuation is needed. If one or multiple complete sentences follow an incomplete caption, each sentence has the appropriate closing punctuation.

| Harvard University graduation ceremony, 2008 |

Formal titles. Generally speaking, titles of most works of art are capitalized in headline style and italicized…whether alone or incorporated into a caption.

| Auguste Rodin, *The Thinker* |

Caption with number. Illustration numbers can be separated from the caption by a period. If the number is typographically distinct, it may be separated by a space.

> Fig 3. Child behavior

Identifying placement. If a caption does not fit on the same page as the illustration, use explanatory wording (placed in italics if needed). The caption should appear at the foot or head of the closest text page.

> *Opposite*: Dynamics of chain reactions

Identifying parts of an illustration. Terms such as *left*, *right*, *top*, *bottom*, *left to right*, *clockwise*, etc. are often used in captions to identify subjects within single illustrations or within single illustrations or parts of a composite. The term is italicized and followed by a comma. If, however, a list follows, use a colon.

> *Above left*, Dr. Robert Williams; *above right*, Dr. Henry Birch; *below left*, Dr. Susan Tienken; *below right*, Dr. Jane Letica

Credit Lines

Source. A credit line, otherwise known as a short statement of the source of an illustration, is generally appropriate and sometimes required. Illustrations created by the author are an exception. A phrase such as *Photo by author* (set in roman) is appropriate.

Permissions. Whether published or unpublished, material under copyright generally requires permission from the copyright owner.

Placement. Credit lines generally appear at the end of a caption. They are placed in parentheses or in different type. A photographer's name will sometimes be placed in small type located parallel to the bottom or side of a photograph.

Form. The language, or form, of a credit line is dependent on its placement and the type and copyright status of the illustration. Credit lines generally follow a consistent pattern within a work.

Author's own material. Illustrations created by the author do not require credit lines. However, a phrase such as *Photo by author* (set in roman) is appropriate if other illustrations in the same work require credit.

Material obtained free of charge. The term *courtesy* (set in roman) may be used for material that has been obtained free of charge and without use restrictions.

Material requiring permission. An illustration reproduced from a published work under copyright protection requires formal permission…unless fair use applies. The credit line should include a page or figure number, along with the author, title, publication details, and (if available) copyright date.

Illustrations: Credit Lines

Material in the public domain. While a credit line is appropriate, illustrations from works in the public domain may be reproduced without permission.

Adapted material. If an author uses data from another source or adjusts the data from another source, credit for the originating source should be granted.

Charts

Essential properties. A chart should be used only if it summarizes the data more appropriately than written words. The chart should be displayed in a relatively simple and comprehensible graphic form.

Consistency. Charts must abide by a consistent style in both graphics and typography when two or more are utilized within a particular work.

Illustrations: Charts

Graphs: the axes. Both the x (horizontal) and y (vertical) axes must be appropriately labeled. The y axis label is read from the bottom up.

Graphs: the curves. Curves should be presented in graphically distinct forms…a continuous line, broken line, etc. All elements should be identified in a caption or in a key.

Labels in relation to captions. The title of a chart is identified in the caption below the chart in printed works.

Abbreviations. Abbreviations and symbols are allowed in labels provided that they are recognizable or described in a key or in the caption.

Main Parts of a Table (See table example at the end of this section)

Table Number

Form. All tables are given an arabic numeral and should be cited directly or parenthetically in the text by the number.

Tabular matter not requiring a number. A short list requiring only two columns does not need to be numbered or titled.

Number sequence. Table numbers follow the order in which the actual tables are placed in the text.

Table Title

Length. The title of a table should briefly identify the contents of the table.

Syntax. The title should be developed in noun form.

Capitalization. Table titles are capitalized in sentence format.

Parenthetical information. Significant explanatory or statistical information can be included in parentheses within the title.

Number plus title. The number of a table should precede the title of the table. Both the number and title should appear on the same line.

Column Heads

Treatment. Column heads should be brief and developed in sentence format.

Explanatory tags. An explanatory tag or subheading is sometimes included in the column head. The tag, either a symbol or abbreviation, is placed in parentheses.

Numbered columns. When columns require numbers for text reference, Arabic numerals should be placed in parentheses. The number and parentheses should be centered immediately below the column head and above the line separating the head from the actual column.

The Stub

Definition. The stub is the left-hand column of a table. It is generally a vertical list of categories that are further explained in the respective table columns.

Stub entries and subentries. Items in the stub may be a sequential or classified list. If a subentry is required, (just like with a main entry) the first word is capitalized. This capitalization will avoid confusion that might result with runover lines.

Typographic treatment of subentries. Subentries must be clearly identified from main entries and runover lines. Subentries may be indented. Alternatively, italics may be used for the main entries while roman may be used for the subentries.

Runover lines. When no subentries are utilized, runover lines are indented one em. Runovers can be placed flush left if there is extra space between rows.

Abbreviations and the like. If space is limited, symbols or abbreviations are acceptable in the stub portion of the table. However, ditto marks are not permissible.

Totals. Indent the word *total* if used at the end of a stub. It can be indented deeper than the greatest indentation found within the table, or it may be distinguished typographically.

The Body and the Cells

Table body. The body of a table is comprised of information in columns to the right of the stub and below the column heading. Cells are spaces within columns. Generally, the cells contain data; however, they sometimes are empty.

Column data. Individual columns should hold the same types of information. For example, dollar values might be in one column and percentages in another column.

Empty cells. If a column head is not applicable to one of the stub entries, the cell may be left blank, filled in with an em dash, or filled in with three unspaced ellipsis dots.

Horizontal alignment. Cells align horizontally to respective stub entries.

Vertical alignment: with column head. Column heads are centered on the longest cell entry. However, the stub head and all stub entries are aligned to the left.

Vertical alignment: numerals. Columns comprised of numerals without commas or decimal points are aligned on the last number.

Vertical alignment: words. When columns are comprised of words, phrases, or sentences, visual appearance determines vertical alignment. If there are no runover lines, entries may be centered. If entries are long, they may begin flush left.

Zeros before decimal points. Zeros are generally added before the decimal point with numbers less than 1.00. In tables, however, they may be omitted if preferred.

Totals, averages, means: typographic treatment. Additional vertical space or short lines periodically appear above totals at the end of columns. However, they are not required. No lines should appear above averages or means.

When to use totals. Totals and subtotals may or may not be included in the table. If useful to the presentation of the data, they may be desirable.

Signs and symbols. In columns exclusively consisting of signs or symbols, the signs or symbols are omitted from the individual cells and included in the column head.

Table 6.1 Sample First-year Program of Study				
Quarter Taken[1]	Seminar Number	Seminar Title	Credits	Grade[2] Received
Year 1				
Quarter 1	BUS 800	Doctoral Seminar in Information Proficiency	2	
	BUS 801	The Scholar Practitioner	4	
Quarter 2	BUS 810	Leading 21st Century Organizations	4	
	BUS 890	Portfolio Development I	2	
Quarter 3	BUS 813	Quality and Organizational Change	4	
	BUS 891	Portfolio Development II	2	
Quarter 4	BUS 811	Managing in a World-Wide Context	4	
	BUS 892	Comprehensive Essay	2	
During Yr 1	BUS 880	Professional Residency	2	

[1] Enter the actual/planned quarter taken. For example, Spring 2008.
[2] Enter your grade upon completion of the seminar.

Mathematical Expressions
General Usage

Standards for mathematical copy. Mathematical copy should be printed clearly and grammatically correct…just as all other printed copy in the document.

Consistency of notation. The use of symbols should be consistent, and the same symbol should denote the same meaning throughout the entire document.

Words versus symbols in text. Mathematical symbols should not be used as replacement for words in a document.

Concise expression. Do not use mathematical symbols unnecessarily.

Sentence beginning with a mathematical symbol. Do not begin a sentence with a mathematical symbol. Simply reword the sentence to make the symbol appear in a different sentence location.

Adjacent mathematical symbols. Separate adjacent mathematical expressions by words or punctuation.

Signs and Symbols

Functions. A function associates a domain with a codomain.

$f : A{\rightarrow}B$ where f is a function from a domain A into a codomain B

Punctuation

Mathematical expressions and punctuation. Mathematical expressions should be punctuated as a sentence or as parts of a sentence.

$$x_1 + x_2 = -7$$

Delimiters

Common delimiters or fences. Mathematical expressions are often grouped by three types of symbols: parentheses ( ), brackets [ ], and braces { }. They are used in pairs and generally in the following sequence: parentheses, brackets, and braces.

Ordered set notation. Use parentheses to delimit an ordered set of objects.

(d,e)

where *d* is the first element in the pair and *e* is the second element

Intervals. Parentheses are used to delimit an open interval; brackets are used to delimit a closed interval.

(d,e)

Denotes the set of all real numbers between *d* and *e* but does not include *d* or *e*.

[d,e]

Denotes the set all real numbers between *d* and *e* and also includes *d* and *e*.

(d,e]

Denotes an interval not including *d* but including *e*.

[d,e)

Denotes an interval including *d* but not including *e*.

Summations and Integrals

Summation sign. The summation sign is used for a sum of finite or infinite terms.

$$\sum(a,b,c) = a+b+c$$

Fractions

Fractions in text. Use a slash to separate the numerator and denominator. If fractions follow a mathematical symbol or expression, they should be placed in parentheses.

| 1/5, 2/3, 3/5 | (c/d)x   x(b/c) |

Abbreviations

General Comments

Periods. Use periods with abbreviations that are written in lowercase letters. However, do not use periods with abbreviations that appear in full capitals or small capitals…regardless of the amount of letters utilized.

Spacing or no spacing between elements. Regardless of lowercase or capitals, do not leave a space between the letters of initialisms and acronyms.

Upper versus lowercase. Noun forms are generally uppercase; adverbial forms are generally lowercase.

Ampersands. When used with an initialism, no space is left on either side of an ampersand.

Names and Titles

Personal names. Generally speaking, abbreviations are not used for given names. However, a signature can be transcribed as the person wrote it.

Initials in personal names. A period and a space are placed after initials representing a given name. Even if the middle initial does not stand for a name, a period is generally utilized.

J. F. Kennedy	P. R. Caldwell

Titles before names. Civil or military titles that precede a full name can be abbreviated. However, if preceding a surname alone, the title is spelled out.

Rep. Jerry Birdwell	Senator Robertson

Military titles. If common to the reader, use full capitals for the abbreviated forms of military ranks.

CPT	COL	GEN

Social titles. Regardless of whether the title precedes the full name or the surname only, always abbreviate.

Dr.	Mr.	Mrs.	Ms.

Reverend/Honorable. When using *the, Reverend* and *Honorable* are spelled out. However, use the abbreviations *Rev.* and *Hon.* when no *the* precedes the title.

Rev. Nancy W.Carey	the Honorable Emma Wackerly

Jr., Sr., and the like. Abbreviations such as *Jr.* as well as roman or arabic numerals such as *III* or *3ʳᵈ* after a person's name are part of the individual's name. As such, they are retained with any given title. Only use abbreviations when the full name is provided, not just the surname.

Mr. Curtis C. Reynolds, Jr.	Dr. William Delosh, III

Academic degrees. Unless needed for tradition or consistency, omit periods included with academic degrees. However, when following an individual's name, some professional, religious, and other designations are set off by commas.

Rosemarie S. Stemmer, PhD	Steven Utech, DDS

Commonly used generic abbreviations. Some commonly used generic abbreviations include the following:

Assoc.	Bros.	Corp.	Ltd.	Mfg.

Company names. In notes, bibliographies, tabular matter, etc., abbreviations and ampersands for company names are acceptable.

Agencies and Organizations

Associations and the like. Abbreviations that are either acronyms or initialisms appear in full capitals and without periods.

Broadcasting companies. No periods are used after call letters of radio stations and television channels.

ABC	NATO	NBC

Saints. When space is limited, do not spell out the word Saint before the name of a Christian saint. Instead, the abbreviation *St.* should be utilized. However, is ample space is available, the entire word (Saint) may be spelled out.

Geographical Terms

U.S. states. The two-letter (no-period) state abbreviation should be used when following the name of a city. However, when the state stands alone (other than DC), it should be spelled out in full.

Detroit, MI		Michigan

Canadian provinces and territories. Canadian provinces and territories can be abbreviated in bibliographies, but they should be spelled out in text.

Names of Countries

When to abbreviate. Country names are spelled out. However, they may be abbreviated in tabular matter, lists, and the like.

"U.S." or "US." U.S. typically appears with periods; however, periods may be omitted. *United States* used as a noun should be spelled out; when used as an adjective, it can be abbreviated.

Compass Points, Latitude, and Longitude

Compass points. Points of the compass may be abbreviated (unless using a mailing address).

N	E	S	W

When not to abbreviate. Never abbreviate the words *latitude* and *longitude*.

Designations of Time

Months. When space is limited, names of months may be abbreviated.

Feb.	Apr.	Dec.

Days of the week. When space is limited, days of the week may be abbreviated.

Tues. or Tu	Fri. or F	Sat. or Sa

Time of the day. If using small capitals, no periods are necessary. Typically the following abbreviations are utilized:

a.m. or AM	p.m. or PM

Avoiding Plagiarism

Plagiarism is a growing problem in educational institutions both domestically and internationally. The word *plagiarize* is defined in *Merriam Webster's Collegiate Dictionary* (10th edition) as, "to steal and pass off (the ideas or words of another) as one's own" (888).

Plagiarism can take one of two forms: intentional or unintentional. When a writer knowingly uses other authors' works without providing appropriate reference citations, he or she is intentionally plagiarizing. If, on the other hand, a writer uses others' thoughts or ideas and does not realize that credit must be provided, he or she is guilty of unintentional plagiarism. Unfortunately, both types of mistakes can result in serious academic consequences. When plagiarism occurs, some institutions may require that the student receive a failing assignment grade; others may insist on a failing course grade; others may place the student on academic probation; and, in extreme cases, some institutions may actually expel the student.

It is incumbent on the writer to be forthright and honest with regard to using original and/or existing writing. Plagiarism can be easily avoided if the writer simply provides appropriate credit when borrowing ideas or citing directly from another individual's work.

When paraphrasing (rewording) work from another author, the writer must provide credit to the person who developed the original work. This simply acknowledges the fact that the paraphrased material was the work of another individual. It is not primary data (original); rather it is secondary data (information already in existence).

Likewise, when citing a direct quote, appropriate credit must be given as well. Again, this signifies that the quote is provided by another individual. When citing verbatim (using another person's exact wording), the borrowed material must be placed in quotation marks and properly cited.

Part Three
Source Citation

Source Documentation Systems

The two basic documentation systems for citing sources are the (1) *notes and bibliography* system and (2) *author-date* system. Essentially, the goal of either system is to give credit to deserving authors and allow readers to locate published or unpublished material utilized within the writing. Both systems are discussed for clarification and understanding.

The notes and bibliography system (humanities style) is used by writers in the arts, history, and literature. Information that is paraphrased, summarized, or quoted is cited by footnotes or endnotes that are typically supplemented with a bibliography. Footnotes are placed in-text at the bottom or "foot" of the page where the citation occurs. Endnotes are placed collectively at the end of the paper. Footnotes and endnotes are designated with a raised arabic numeral that immediately follows the work being recognized (the numerals are full sized, not raised, in the notes themselves), and these numerals are listed in consecutive order, beginning with 1, throughout the paper. If endnotes and footnotes are both used in the same document, endnotes are referenced with numbers and footnotes are referenced with symbols (asterisks, daggers, parallels, etc.). Footnotes and endnotes referring to tables or other non-textual matter are numbered independently (using letters) from those referring to textual matter.

The bibliography provides an overview of utilized sources and lists works cited on a separate page. If there is no bibliography or the bibliography contains only a selected list, then full details (including page number) are given in the footnotes or endnotes at first mention of any work cited. Footnotes and endnotes are concise if the bibliography contains complete details of all works in order to avoid duplication of information. This system is excellent for a diverse assortment of sources, including those that are obscure or inappropriate for the author-date system.

The *author-date* system is used by writers in the natural, physical, and social sciences. Paraphrased, summarized, or quoted sources are cited in text, typically in parentheses, using the author's surname(s), publication date, and page numbers (if necessary). Complete details of the sources are listed in the *Reference List*. This system works best when sources can be easily converted to author-date citations. Other sources, such as manuscripts and anonymous works, are typically better referred to in footnotes and endnotes.

Both source documentation systems can be combined if necessary. For example, a paper utilizing mostly footnotes and endnotes can include some parenthetical citations in text, and a paper following the author-date methodology can contain some notes.

Footnotes and Endnotes
Footnotes

Footnotes

- Footnotes are sometimes preferred over endnotes because all pertinent information is available on the same page.

- Readers of scholarly work often prefer footnotes to endnotes due to ease of reference.

- A superscripted arabic numeral in text represents a word, sentence, phrase, or quotation from another source.

- The superscripted arabic numeral in text should appear as close as possible to the word, sentence, phrase, or quotation that it represents, but it is sometimes best to place it at the end of the sentence to minimize confusion.

Acceptable
Michael Visconti's most recent book, "Walking with International Superstars: Life as a Professional Sports Agent,"[1] was published over three years ago.

Preferable
Michael Visconti's most recent book, "Walking with International Superstars: Life as a Professional Sports Agent," was published over three years ago.[1]

- The superscripted numbers in text run consecutively throughout the document or start new with each chapter.

- There is no space between the superscripted arabic numeral in text and the word, sentence, phrase, or quotation.

- Place corresponding entries at the foot (or bottom) of the page where the source is referenced in text.

- Entries at the bottom of a page must correspond with reference numbers in text.

- If text runs short on a page (such as at the end of a chapter), the entry should still be placed at the bottom of the page.

- If an entry is too long for one page, it should be completed at the bottom of the next page. However, all footnotes should at least begin on the page on which they are referenced.

- Indent the first line of each entry at the bottom of the page three spaces from the left margin. The following lines are flush with left margin.

Footnotes

- Single space each entry at the bottom of the page, and double space between entries.

- A *footnote* feature is available on many word processing programs (such as Microsoft Word).

In the military, publicly berating a subordinate in order to achieve positive behavioral change is accepted.[1] A boot camp drill sergeant, for example, may scream at a new recruit and call him or her derogatory names because her or his bed was not made properly. This type of verbal abuse would probably not be accepted if a hotel manager were to reprimand a maid in a similar manner for the same infraction.[2]

---

1. Anthony J. Bonanno, *Argumentative Strategies in the Military*, (Chicago: Sinclair Books, 2008), 212.

2. Margaret Lapensee, *Hotel Etiquette: A Training Guide for Management*, (New York: Leodan Books, 2008), 17–18.

Endnotes

- Endnotes are sometimes preferred over footnotes because they leave pages looking less cluttered.

- Tables, quoted poetry, and similar matter are preferably listed in endnotes instead of footnotes.

- A superscripted arabic numeral in text represents a word, sentence, phrase, or quote.

- The superscripted arabic numeral in text should appear as close as possible to the word, sentence, phrase, or quote that it represents, but it is sometimes best to place it at the end of the sentence to minimize confusion. See the *footnote* section for an example.

- The superscripted numbers in text run consecutively throughout the document or start new with each chapter.

- There is no space between the superscripted arabic numeral in text and the word, sentence, phrase.

- Place corresponding entries on a separate *notes* page at the end of a chapter or end of a document.

- Entries on the notes page must correspond with reference numbers in text.

- The notes page contains the heading *Notes*, which is centered at the top of the page.

- Double space between the heading and the first entry on the notes page.

- Indent the first line of each entry on the notes page three spaces from the left margin. The following lines are flush with left margin.

- Single space each entry on the notes page, and double space between entries.

- An *endnote* feature is available on many word processing programs (such as Microsoft Word).

Notes

1. Art Kerkau, and Carol Creisher, *Changing Times on Kingston Avenue*, (Huntington Woods, MI: Axel & Joyce , 2008), 29–31.

2. Lacy M. Gardner, "Change and Suburban Neighborhoods: A Qualitative Analysis," *Change Management* 27, no. 4 (2008): 175.

3. Ibid., 181.

4. D'Andre Sims, "Suburban Renewal: Inside a Conservative Bedroom Community," *Newsweek*, July 19, 2008, 22.

In General (Footnotes and Endnotes)

Footnotes and Endnotes

- List as they occur (not alphabetically like bibliographies and reference lists).

- Authors (editors, compilers, or translators) are listed as they appear on the sources (in the first reference; in subsequent references, list only the surname).

- Authors' (editors', compilers', or translators') given names are used instead of initials if known unless those individuals prefer initials (in the first reference; in subsequent references, list only the surname).

- Titles of work appear in full in the first reference and are shortened in subsequent references (using key words) if the titles contain more than four words. Shortened titles contain key words from full titles and wording order is not changed.

- Publication dates appear after the publishers (in the first reference only).

- Page numbers are not listed if the work is being referred to as a whole.

- Page numbers are not listed for books unless citing specific chapters or passages.

- Beginning and ending page numbers of articles are listed for journals when referencing the article as a whole. In referring to a specific passage, only those page numbers are listed.

- Page numbers are listed for electronic sources (if available).

- Electronic sources list pages, sections, equations, or other divisions of work if available. If not available (which is often the case), list nothing.

- Titles of books and names of journals are italicized.

Footnotes and Endnotes

- Titles of articles, chapters, and poems are placed in quotation marks.

- Titles of books, articles, and journal names are capitalized headline style (lower and uppercase lettering).

- Paragraph indents (within the same footnote or endnote) are avoided to prevent confusion.

- Footnotes and endnotes may contain citations plus commentary; however, complicated information (lists, tabular material, etc.) is placed in the appendix section.

- If more than ten abbreviations of titles, names, manuscript collections, etc. are used, then they are listed along with the unabbreviated form in alphabetical order in a separate section headed *Abbreviations*.

- If there are two or three authors, all are listed in the first and subsequent references.

- If there are more than three authors, list all of them in the first reference, then list the first author followed by *et al.* or *and others* in subsequent references.

1 through 4 are examples of cited sources, and 5 through 8 are examples of shortened forms of subsequent citations for the same sources:

1. Isaiah F. Trimble, *Poverty in Russia: Repercussions of Industrialization* (New York: Citadel Press, 2008).

2. Martin R. Prasko, "Total Quality Control in Scientific Research," *Quality Quarterly* 22, no. 3 (2008): 132–47.

3. Chontrella Watkins, *West Coast Underworld: Confessions of a San Diego Business Mogul,* ed. T. R. Reinhold (Chicago: University of Illinois Press, 2007).

4. Joseph A. McCracken, Scott McCauley, David Sikorski, and T. J. Foyer, "Troubled Teens: Research in a Pittsburgh Youth Home," *Journal of Adolescent Behavior* 12, no. 4 (2007): 112–14.

5. Trimble, *Poverty in Russia.*

6. Prasko, "Total Quality Control," 140, 142.

7. Watkins, *West Coast Underworld*, 161.

8. McCracken et al., "Troubled Teens," 112–19.

Footnotes and Endnotes

- The word *Ibid.* refers to the immediately preceding endnote or footnote by taking the place of all the required information.

- List a page number if different than the immediately preceding endnote or footnote page number.

3. Chantal, *Walking in Heaven*, 312.

4. Ibid., 261–63.

- Quotations are in quotation marks followed by the source.

1. Reed states: "The system is designed to withstand a harsh environment." *Computer Hardware*, Terrell M. Jones (Philadelphia: Philadelphia College Press, 2008), 229.

- Footnotes continuing on another page must break in mid-sentence to avoid missing the end of the note.

Bottom of page 12

16. Johansen noted the following during her diagnosis: "We don't always know why things happen, but we can often make reasonable guesses based on the psychological

Bottom of page 13

and physiological information available to us." *Modern Science*, Alice Tumbrollo (Detroit: University of Detroit Press, 2008), 301.

Footnotes and Endnotes

- Endnotes for a book are placed together, after the text and appendixes and before the bibliography. The main heading is *Notes*, and the notes for each chapter are introduced with that chapter as a subheading. However, if a book has different authors for each chapter, then the endnotes are placed at the end of each chapter under a *Notes* heading.

(Assume the text portion of the document ends here)

Notes

Chapter One

1. The situation in England signaled a need for change, and that is why the ruling monarchy made decisions that were questionable at the time. See Robert Marfachuk, *Fateful Decisions of English Rulers*, (Atlanta: Williamsburg, 2007), 174.

2. Nelson notes: "London had its own share of problems during that revolutionary period." *European History*, John Taggworth (Boston: University of Boston Press, 2008), 207.

> Chapter Two
>
> 1. Daniel Grady Wilson specified: "The English tradition must be upheld under the worst of circumstances." *Monarchies*, Mark Otto (Las Vegas: University of Nevada Press, 2008), 11.

- Endnotes in journals are placed at the end of each article under a *Notes* heading.

Bibliographies

- This section is similar, but not identical, to the *Reference* or *Works Cited* section in the *author-date* system.

- Bibliographies are used with footnotes or endnotes.

- Full bibliographies include all cited works (books, articles, and other references). The heading of a full bibliography is *Bibliography*.

- Selected bibliographies contain only the most important works cited and contain a head note explaining the reasoning for selection. The heading of a selected bibliography is *Selected Bibliography*.

- Single space individual bibliography entries and double space between each entry.

- Bibliography entries use the hanging indent feature. The first line of each entry is flush left and the following lines are indented.

- References are listed in alphabetical order by authors (using surname of first author), associations (if the work is authored by an organization), or place or thing (if work is anonymous).

- Authors are listed alphabetically by surnames. If no author is provided, the entries are alphabetized according to the first word of the title (ignore *A, An,* or *The*).

- Multiple author entries invert the first author's name and list subsequent authors as written.

> Markell, William Maynard, Andrea M. Jameson, and
> Marlene Thompson. "Living Dinosaurs: Wall Street's
> Last Hurrah." *Business Review* 23 (1998): 311–18.

- Multiple authors with the same surname are listed alphabetically by first name.

> Jones, Amos. "The Fate of the Archdiocese: A Qualitative
> Analysis." *Religious Quarterly* 21 (2007): 12–19.
>
> Jones, Martin. *Walking with Giants*. New York: Doubleday,
> 2008.
>
> Jones, N. D. "Happiness of the Soul." In *Survival of the Fittest:
> A Historical Perspective*, edited by Gregory Porter,
> 291–312. Chicago: University of Chicago Press, 2008.

Bibliographies

- Successive entries by authors with different co-authors are listed alphabetically by the first author's surname, followed by the alphabetical listing of the co-author's surnames.

> Crocenzi, Lawrence. *Professional Football: The Formative
> Years*. 2nd ed. Chicago: Rand McNally, 2006.
>
> Crocenzi, Lawrence, and Raymond K. Dempz.
> *Professional Football: Game Changes*. Chicago:
> Rand McNally, 2008.
>
> Crocenzi, Lawrence, Dino Simone, and Jerome Williams.
> *Professional Football: America's Favorite Pastime*.
> Chicago: Rand McNally, 2007.

- Successive entries by the same author(s), editor(s), compiler(s), translator(s), institution(s), or corporate author(s) use a 3-em dash to replace the author(s), editor(s), compiler(s), translator(s), institution(s), or corporate author(s) after the first listing. The 3-em dash is followed by a period or comma, as was listed in the previous entry. Titles are listed alphabetically (ignore *A, An,* or *The*).

Authors

Wirtanen, David R., Paul G. Bonder, and T. M. Stralicki. *Basics of Auto Racing.* Los Angeles: Markem, 2007.

_____. "The Stress of Racing." In *Modern Automotive Concepts*, edited by Bernard T. Brock, 291–306. Los Angeles: Markem, 2006.

Editors

Terelli, Samantha P., Joan L. Montrose, and Kelly R. Simpson, eds. *Intermediate Mathematics in American High Schools.* Cincinnati: University of Cincinnati Press, 2007.

_____. *Simple Mathematics in American Middle Schools.* Cincinnati: University of Cincinnati Press, 2008.

Institutions

U. S. Senate. Committee on Immigration. *Determining Legality.* 75th Cong., 2nd sess., 1921.

_____. *Immigrant Responsibility.* 84th Cong., 3rd sess., 1931.

Bibliographies

- Authors' (editors', compilers', or translators') given names are used instead of initials if known, unless those individuals prefer initials.

- Authors' initials used in place of a given name are listed before spelled-out names beginning with the same letter.

- Acronyms, abbreviations, and initialisms are listed as they appear, not as fully spelled out.

- Publication dates appear after the publishers.

- Page numbers are not listed for books unless citing specific chapters.

- Beginning and ending page numbers of articles are listed for journals.

- Page numbers are listed for electronic sources (if available).

- Numerals are listed as spelled out.

- Titles of books and names of journals are italicized.

- Titles of articles, chapters, and poems are placed in quotation marks.

- Titles of books, articles, and journal names are capitalized headline style.

- *A, An,* or *The* (introductory words) in titles, associations, places, or organizations are omitted.

Bibliographies

The University of Michigan	*is listed as*	University of Michigan
The Timberland Group	*is listed as*	Timberland Group
The Netherlands	*is listed as*	Netherlands
The Bronx	*is listed as*	Bronx

- Personal names used as names of organizations or associations are listed as written.

E. F. Hutton & Co.	*is listed as*	E. F. Hutton & Co.
T. J. Maxx	*is listed as*	T. J. Maxx

- Names of mountains and lakes are inverted and listed under the non-generic names.

Lake Michigan	*is listed as*	Michigan, Lake
Mount Everest	*is listed as*	Everest, Mount

- Names of cities and islands beginning with topographical elements are listed as such.

Lake Placid, NY	*is listed as*	Lake Placid, NY
Mt. Pleasant, MI	*is listed as*	Mt. Pleasant, MI
Isle of Wight	*is listed as*	Isle of Wight

- Bibliographies precede the index at the end of a document. However, textbooks and multi-authored books have bibliographies at the end of each chapter.

Parenthetical Citations (author-date system)

- Parenthetical citations are used in text to direct readers to the reference list for full details.

- Authors, publication dates, page numbers (if necessary), volume numbers, sections, and comments are listed. When authors' names appear in text, they need not be repeated in parenthetical citation.

Parenthetical Citations

Author and date
(Romano 2007) *or* Romano (2007)

Author, date, and page number (comma after date)
(Jackson 2006, 85) *or* Jackson (2006, 85)

Author, date, and volume (comma after date)
(Sheckle 2008, vol. 3) *or* Sheckle (2008, vol. 3)

Author, date, volume, and page number (comma after date, colon after volume)
(Porter 2007, 2:324) *or* Porter (2007, 2:324)

Author, date, volume, and section (comma after date)
(Marcette 2005, sec. 22) *or* Marcette (2005, sec. 22)

Author, date, and comment (comma after date)
(Kayster 2008, arithmetic mean used) *or* Kayster (2008, arithmetic mean used)

- Different authors with the same surname use initials to distinguish (two initials are necessary if the first initials are the same).

(D. Wasniak 2007)	(K. Wasniak 2008)

- Authors with two or more works in the same year are denoted by lowercase letters *a*, *b*, *c*, etc. after the date. Letters are listed in the order the citations fall in the document (alphabetical order does not apply). Use *and* (not *&*) to separate authors.

> (Macklin and McDowell 2006a)
>
> (Macklin and McDowell 2006b)

- If there are more than three authors, then list only the first author followed by *et al.* or *and others*.

> (Kurtz et al. 2007)
>
> A study by Kurtz and others (2007) found dogs to be more aggressive than cats.
>
> *or*
>
> A study by Kurtz et al. (2007) found dogs to be more aggressive than cats.

Parenthetical Citations

- Two or more references within parentheses are separated by semi-colons. These references can be listed by importance, chronological order, or alphabetical order.

> (Smithers 2008; Jones and Williams 2007; Pinkly et al. 2005)

- There must be a reference listing for every parenthetical citation.
- Page numbers are necessary if referring to specific passages.
- Electronic sources list pages, sections, or other divisions of work if available. If not available (which is often the case), list nothing.

Reference Lists (author-date system)

- This section is similar, but not identical to, the bibliographies section in the notes and bibliography system. It is used with the author-date system.
- Alphabetizing rules follow those in the bibliographies section.

- There must be a parenthetical citation in text for every reference list citation.

- Single space individual reference list entries and double space between each entry.

- Reference list entries use the hanging indent feature. The first line of each entry is flush left and the following lines are indented.

- Publication dates immediately follow the authors' (editors', compilers', or translators') names.

- Multiple author entries invert the first author's name and list subsequent authors as written.

- Successive entries by the same author(s), editor(s), compiler(s), translator(s), institution(s), or corporate author(s) follow the rules listed in the bibliographies section (using the 3-em dash).

- Authors with two or more works in the same year are denoted by *a, b, c*, etc. after the date. Entries are alphabetized by title in the Reference List.

Symzyk, Gregory M. 2008b. *Advanced racquetball techniques: Strategies for success*. Ithaca, NY: Barden Books.

Symzyk, Gregory M. 2008a. *Racquetball techniques for beginners*. Ithaca, NY: Barden Books.

- Authors' (editors', compilers', or translators') initials can be used instead of full names if only initials are given (this is not uncommon in the natural sciences).

- Authors' initials used in place of a given name are listed before spelled-out names beginning with the same letter.

- Publication dates are placed after the authors, editors, translators, or compilers.

Tisdelle, Kathleen R., and Terry Taylor. 2007. *Adult friendships and adult socialization*. Cambridge, MA: MIT Press.

Reference Lists

- Page numbers are not listed for books unless citing specific chapters.
- Beginning and ending page numbers are listed for journal articles.
- Page numbers are listed for electronic sources (if available).
- Titles of books and names of journals are italicized.
- Titles of articles, chapters, and poems are not italicized.
- Journal names are capitalized headline style, and titles of books and articles are capitalized sentence style.

Headline style (journal)
Journal of Social Relationships
Sentence style (book)
Building a model wooden ship: The search for perfection

Reference Lists

- Reference lists precede the index at the end of a document. However, textbooks and multi-authored books have reference lists at the end of each chapter, in which case the list is subheaded *References* or *Literature Cited*.
- Journals listing months are abbreviated.

Month	*Acceptable abbreviation*
January	Jan.
February	Feb.

- Science journal titles are abbreviated using the *Index Medicus* (use an Internet search engine to find *Index Medicus*) or the *BIOSIS Serial Sources* (use an Internet search engine to find *BIOSIS Serial Sources*).
- Other abbreviations are as listed below.

Phrase	*Acceptable abbreviation*
Edited by	ed. (capitalized if following a period)
Translated by	trans. (capitalized if following a period)
University	Univ.

Coding System

The Chicago Manual of Style (15th edition) uses the following key to designate examples for the two types of source documentation systems:

N = Footnotes or Endnotes (notes and bibliography system)

B = Bibliography (notes and bibliography system)

T = Parenthetical citation (author-date system)

R = Reference list (author-date system)

For ease of reference, the same key will be used in this book. The following are examples of how to properly cite sources:

Books

List Entries in the Following Order:

Author(s) – list editor(s) or institution if no author is listed

Title – also list subtitle if applicable

Editor(s), Compiler(s), or Translator(s) – if listed in addition to the author(s)

Edition – if it is not the first

Volume – list individual number if single volume is cited and total number if referred to as a whole

Series – list volume number within series if series is numbered

Publication city – list state if necessary

Publisher

Publication date

Page number(s) – if applicable

URL (for Internet or other electronic sources)

Medium (DVD, CD-ROM, etc.) – if not a book

In General

• Titles are italicized.

• Titles in bibliographies, footnotes, and endnotes are capitalized headline style, and titles in *reference lists* are capitalized sentence style.

• Titles in full capital letters are changed to lower and uppercase letters (following the appropriate headline or sentence style) unless they are acronyms or initialisms.

- Italicized terms within titles (such as names of bacteria in scientific research) use roman type (reverse italics).

> *Research methodology for the study of* Listeria monocytogenes *in prepared salads*

- *Ampersands* (&) in titles are changed to *and*.

- Subtitles are separated by a colon and the first letter is capitalized (both headline and sentence style).

> *Headline style*
> B: The Mad Doctor: A Story about Truth in Medicine.
>
> *Sentence style*
> R: The mad doctor: A story about truth in medicine.

Books

Publication Facts for Footnotes, Endnotes, Bibliographies, and Reference Lists

- Publication cities must include states (and provinces or countries) if the cities are not well known or can be confused with cities of the same name in different states.

Chicago	New York	Baltimore
Port Austin, MI	Reading, PA	Wooster, OH
London	Paris	Mexico City
Waterloo, ON	Sainte-Foy, QC	Alba, Italy

- Publication states are not used if they appear in the publisher names.

> Brookings: South Dakota State University Press

- Unknown publication places list *n.p.* (*N.p.* if after a period) as the place of publication.

- Unknown publication dates follow same procedure as publication places, but list *n.d.* or *N.d.* as the date of publication.

N: 1. Roberta Dimas, *Retail Giants: The Greatest American Men Ever* (n.p.: Morton, 1911).

B: Dimas, Roberta. *Retail Giants: The Greatest American Men Ever.* N.p.: Morton, 1911.

- Omit *The* from the beginning of publisher's names.
- Omit *Inc.* and *Ltd.* from publisher's names.
- Retain *Books* in publisher's names.
- Retain *Press* if listed in the name of a university press or newspaper, but omit it if listed in the name of a company.

Books

The Hartford	*is listed as*	Hartford
Felton, Inc.	*is listed as*	Felton
Dimension Books	*is listed as*	Dimension Books
Oakland University Press	*is listed as*	Oakland University Press
San Juan Free Press	*is listed as*	San Juan Free Press
Bosworth Press	*is listed as*	Bosworth

- Publication dates list year only (not month or day).
- Use *forthcoming* for works that are in press with unknown publication dates. Use a comma between authors and *forthcoming* in parenthetical citations. Capitalize *forthcoming* in reference lists only.

N: 2. Jonathon Groebel and Martha Guzzardo, *Changing Times at Maryland Middle Schools* (Baltimore: Paragon, forthcoming).

B: Groebel, Jonathon, and Martha Guzzardo. *Changing Times at Maryland Middle Schools.* Baltimore: Paragon, forthcoming.

T: (Groebel and Guzzardo, forthcoming)

R: Groebel, Jonathon, and Martha Guzzardo. Forthcoming. *Changing times at Maryland middle schools.* Baltimore: Paragon.

- Arabic numerals are typically used for chapters, volumes, and other divisions.

- Ranges of numbers list the first and last numbers.

- Tables and illustrations can use *fig.* for *figure*, but *plate, map*, and other illustration forms are spelled out.

N:	3. Guy E. Hardin, *Eighties Punk Bands: Their Influence on Contemporary Music* (New York: Ratfink Books, 2008), 64, fig. 2.1.

One Author, Editor, Compiler, or Translator

Books

N:	1. Tracy Benson, *Hidden Tragedies of War* (Englewood Cliffs, NJ: Prentice Hall, 2008).
B:	Benson, Tracy. *Hidden Tragedies of War*. Englewood Cliffs, NJ: Prentice Hall, 2008.
T:	(Benson 2008)
R:	Benson, Tracy. 2008. *Hidden tragedies of war*. Englewood Cliffs, NJ: Prentice Hall.

Two Authors, Editors, Compilers, or Translators

- Use *and* (not &) to separate authors.

N:	2. Katherine Bogner and Delores Huff, *Watching Trees Grow: The Real Dirt* (Defiance, OH: Orville Books, 2007).
B:	Bogner, Katherine, and Delores Huff. *Watching Trees Grow: The Real Dirt*. Defiance, OH: Orville Books, 2007.
T:	(Bogner and Huff 2007)
R:	Bogner, Katherine, and Dolores Huff. 2007. *Watching trees grow: The real dirt*. Defiance, OH: Orville Books.

Three Authors, Editors, Compilers, or Translators

N:	3. Warren T. Peschke, Earl Sherwood, and Roger M. Wolverine, *Great Meat Packing Houses in the United States* (Chicago: University of Chicago Press, 2008).
B:	Peschke, Warren T., Earl Sherwood, and Roger M. Wolverine. *Great Meat Packing Houses in the United States*. Chicago: University of Chicago Press, 2008.
T:	(Peschke, Sherwood, and Wolverine 2008)
R:	Peschke, Warren T., Earl Sherwood, and Roger M. Wolverine. 2008. *Great meat packing houses in the United States*. Chicago: University of Chicago Press.

More than Three Authors, Editors, Compilers, or Translators

Books

- Use *et al.* or *and others* for footnotes, endnotes, and parenthetical citations.

- The exception to this is a reference list with sources from the natural sciences. List all authors if there are ten or fewer, and list the first seven if there are eleven or more authors. This follows the *American Naturalist* policy (use an Internet search engine to find *American Naturalist*).

N:	4. James Mickleberry and others, *Duck Hunting in Western Canada* (Baltimore: Pensacola Books, 2007).
B:	Mickleberry, James, Richard L. Jaworski, Mitchell Pitt, and Peter K. Kowalski. *Duck Hunting in Western Canada*. Baltimore: Pensacola Books, 2007.
T:	(Mickleberry et al. 2007)
R:	Mickleberry, James, Richard L. Jaworski, Mitchell Pitt, and Peter K. Kowalski. 2007. *Duck hunting in Western Canada*. Baltimore: Pensacola Books.

Anonymous Works or Unknown Authors

- List alphabetically by title (ignore *A, An,* or *The*).

- The term *Anonymous* is typically avoided, but *Anonymous* or *Anon* can be used in a reference list or bibliography where several anonymous works are grouped together. When listing by *Anonymous* or *Anon,* follow the 3-em dash procedure for successive entries in the bibliographies section.

Editors, Compilers, or Translators in Addition to Authors

- List author(s), title, editor(s), compiler(s), or translator(s).

- *Edited by* can be listed as *ed.* (but not *eds.*), but spell out *edited by* in bibliographies.

- *Compiled by* can be listed at *comp.* (but not *comps.*), but spell out *compiled by* in bibliographies.

Books

- *Translated by* can be listed as *trans.*, but spell out *translated by* in bibliographies.

N:	5. Montreles R. Skropodopolis, *Modern Day Greece*, trans. Richard Borkowski (Cambridge, MA: Harvard University Press, 2008).
B:	Skropodopolis, Montreles R. *Modern Day Greece.* Translated by Richard Borkowski. Cambridge, MA: Harvard University Press, 2008.
T:	(Skropodopolis 2008)
R:	Skropodopolis, Montreles R. 2008. *Modern day Greece.* Trans. Richard Borkowski. Cambridge, MA: Harvard Univ. Press.

Chapters in Books with One Author or Editor

- List author, chapter title (footnotes, endnotes, and bibliographies use quotation marks), book title (in italics), and page numbers or chapter.

N:	6. Cassandra Ellsworth, "The Color of Blue," in *Interior House Decoration*, (Rehoboth Beach, DE: Pony Books, 2008), 221–43.

B:	Ellsworth, Cassandra. "The Color of Blue." Chap. 7 in *Interior House Decoration*. Rehoboth Beach, DE: Pony Books, 2008.
T:	(Ellsworth 2008, 221–43)
R:	Ellsworth, Cassandra. 2008. The color of blue. In *Interior house decoration*, 221–43. Rehoboth Beach, DE: Pony Books.

Contributions to Books with More Than One Author or Editor

- List contributor(s), contribution title (footnotes, endnotes, and bibliographies use quotation marks), book title (italicized), authors or editors, and page numbers.

- This also applies to contributions at a conference.

N:	7. Joel Frederick and Henry Herrud, "Nepotism and Promotion," in *Running a Successful Family Business,* ed. Alexander Hornung (Detroit: Dorfman Books, 2007), 12–18.
B:	Frederick, Joel, and Henry Herrud. "Nepotism and Promotion." In *Running a Successful Family Business,* edited by Alexander Hornung, 12–18. Detroit: Dorfman Books, 2007.
T:	(Frederick and Herrud 2007, 12–18)
R:	Frederick, Joel, and Henry Herrud. 2007. Nepotism and promotion. In *Running a successful family business,* ed. Alexander Hornung, 12–18. Detroit: Dorfman Books.

Afterwords, Forewords, Introductions, or Prefaces by People other than the Author

- List afterword, foreword, introduction, or preface before the title of the book.

N:	8. Melchior Stemmer, forward to *Opening a Bump and Weld Shop*, by Theresa Van Mill (Chicago: Eschner, 2007).

B:	Stemmer, Melchior. Forward to *Opening a Bump and Weld Shop,* by Theresa Van Mill. Chicago: Eschner, 2007.
T:	(Stemmer 2007)
R:	Stemmer, Melchior. 2007. Forward to *Opening a bump and weld shop,* by Theresa Van Mill. Chicago: Eschner.

Editions

Books

N:	9. Henry House, *Politics in the Deep South: The Struggle for Change in Established Venues,* 3rd ed. (Buffalo Grove, IL: Jones and Primmer, 2006).
B:	House, Henry. *Politics in the Deep South: The Struggle for Change in Established Venues.* 3rd ed. Buffalo Grove, IL: Jones and Primmer, 2006.
T:	(House 2006)
R:	House, Henry. 2006. *Politics in the deep south: The struggle for change in established venues.* 3rd ed. Buffalo Grove, IL: Jones and Primmer.

Multi Volumes

- Whole numbers are listed as arabic numerals.
- Omit the word *vol.* if the volume number is followed by a page number.
- When cited as whole volumes, list the total number of volumes after the title or editors' names.
- If published over several years, list the range of years.

N:	10. Martha Zellenac, *Evolution of Polio Vaccination,* ed. James Pratt (Cincinnati: Cincinnati Books, 1991-1999), 3:215.
B:	Zellenac, Martha. *Evolution of Polio Vaccination.* Edited by James Pratt. 4 vols. Cincinnati: Cincinnati Books, 1991-1999.

T:	(Zellenac 2008, 3:215)
R:	Zellenac, Martha. 1991-1999. *Evolution of polio vaccination.* Ed. James Pratt. 4 vols. Cincinnati: Cincinnati Books.

Series

- Series titles are capitalized headline style (no italics or quotation marks) for footnotes, endnotes, bibliographies, and reference lists.

- Series editors are typically omitted.

- Numbers (if available) follow the series title.

N:	11. Rosemary J. Winters, *Famous Mountains: The Himalayas,* Studies of Rugged Terrain 9 (Boston: Shackelford Books, 2008).	**Books**
B:	Winters, Rosemary J. *Famous Mountains: The Himalayas.* Studies of Rugged Terrain 9. Boston: Shackelford Books, 2008.	
T:	(Winters 2008)	
R:	Winters, Rosemary J. 2008. *Famous mountains: The Himalayas.* Studies of Rugged Terrain 9. Boston: Shackelford Books.	

Electronic Books

- Follow the guidelines for printed books.

- In addition to the full facts of publication, list the URL (after the publisher).

- Retrieval or access dates of Internet sites are typically not listed. Exceptions include time-sensitive fields such as law or medicine where small updates or corrections might be important (list after the URL).

- Mediums other than the Internet should be noted.

N: 12. Benjamin Zukowski, *Legal Documents Pertaining to Trade Agreements* (Bedford, TX: Legal Aid, 2007), http://www.legalaid.com/pubs/trade/htmlbook08/ (accessed November 23, 2008).

B: Zukowski, Benjamin. *Legal Documents Pertaining to Trade Agreements.* Bedford, TX: Legal Aid, 2007. http://www.legalaid.com/pubs/trade/htmlbook08/ (accessed November 23, 2008).

T: (Zukowski 2008)

Books

R: Zukowski, Benjamin. 2007. *Legal documents pertaining to trade agreements.* Bedford, TX: Legal Aid. http://www.legalaid.com/pubs/trade/htmlbook08/ (accessed November 23, 2008).

- Non-Internet sources list the medium or format (such as CD-ROM or DVD).

R: Finkleberry, Nelson R. 2008. *Computer skills for beginners: Learning is easy.* Little Rock, AR: Clinton Books. CD-ROM.

Periodicals (Journals, Magazines, and Newspapers)

List Entries in the Following Order:

Periodicals

Author(s)
Article or column title – also list subtitle if applicable
Periodical title
Issue information – volume, issue number, date, etc.
Page number(s) – if applicable
URL (for Internet or other electronic sources)

In General

- Follow the guidelines in the *Books* section for listing authors or editors.

- Bibliographies and reference lists list the first and last page numbers of an article. Footnotes, endnotes, and parenthetical citations list specific article pages unless the entire article is cited.

- Article titles are capitalized headline style (in quotation marks) in footnotes, endnotes, and bibliographies. Article titles are capitalized sentence style in reference lists (quotation marks are not used)

Journals

- Journal titles are italicized and capitalized headline style in footnotes, endnotes, bibliographies, and reference lists.

- Journal titles are listed in full (omitting *The* if it is the first word in the title) in footnotes, endnotes, and bibliographies. Journal titles are often abbreviated in reference lists (especially for scientific works), but this is not mandatory. Abbreviations can be found in the *Periodical Title Abbreviations* (use an Internet search engine to find *Periodical Title Abbreviations*).

Periodicals

N:	1. Theodore M. Funke and David P. Camillari, "Obsolete Accounting Principles Revisited: Expanding the Role of the CPA," *Journal of Accounting Studies* 37 (2008): 147–53.
B:	Funke, Theodore M., and David P. Camillari. "Obsolete Accounting Principles Revisited: Expanding the Role of the CPA." *Journal of Accounting Studies* 37 (2008): 147–53.
T:	(Funke and Camillari 2008, 148)
R:	Funke, Theodore M., and David P. Camillari. 2008. Obsolete accounting principles revisited: Expanding the role of the CPA. *Journal of Accounting Studies* 37:147–53.

- If page numbers follow a volume or issue, there is no space before the colon. However, if parenthetical information intervenes, then a space is placed between the colon and the pages.

> No space before colon
>
> *Journal of Economic Research* 17:221–34
>
> *Education Research* 16, no. 2:84–89
>
> Space before between colon and pages
>
> *Education Quarterly* 23, no. 3 (Spring): 215–31
>
> *Math Review* 15 (August 2007*)*: 112–17

- Volume numbers are placed after journal titles using arabic numerals.

Periodicals

- Issue numbers in footnotes, endnotes, and bibliographies are placed after volume numbers (preceded by *no.*). Issue numbers in reference lists are placed after the volume numbers in parentheses (this is unnecessary when a month or season precedes the year).

- Dates are placed in parentheses after volume numbers or issue numbers in footnotes, endnotes and bibliographies. Dates are placed after the author(s) or editor(s) in reference lists.

- Seasons are capitalized and are not necessary if issue numbers are listed.

> N: 2. Darrel R. Ivankowicz, "Social Skills of Middle School Students in Advanced Math," *Education Quarterly* 21, no. 3 (2007): 215–31.
>
> B: Ivankowicz, Darrel R. "Social Skills of Middle School Students in Advanced Math." *Education Quarterly* 21, no. 3 (2007): 215–31.
>
> T: (Ivankowicz 2007)
>
> R: Ivankowicz, Darrel R. 2007. Social skills of middle school students in advanced math. *Education Quarterly* 21 (3):215–31.

- Italicized terms within article titles remain italicized.

> B: Versailles, Juanita J. "Health Concerns of *Shell-Shocked* Viet Nam Veterans." *Psychology Today* 21 (2006): 396–408.

- Quoted terms within article titles are double quoted in reference lists and single quoted in footnotes, endnotes, and bibliographies.

> B: Collins, Lisa A. "The Influence of 'Dead Man Walking' on Death Row Inmates." *Communication Monographs* 12 (2008):112–17.
>
> R: Collins, Lisa A. 2008. The influence of "Dead Man Walking" on death row inmates. *Communication Monographs* 12:112–17.

- Use *forthcoming* for works that have been accepted for publication in journals, but have not yet appeared. Position *forthcoming* in place of the year and page numbers. Capitalize *forthcoming* in reference lists only.

Periodicals

> N: 3. Samuel T. Lopiccollo, "The Relationship of Injury and Absenteeism in Produce Terminals: A Quantitative Study," *Journal of Human Resources* 19 (forthcoming).
>
> B: Lopiccollo, Samuel T. "The Relationship of Injury and Absenteeism in Produce Terminals: A Quantitative Study." *Journal of Human Resources* 19 (forthcoming).
>
> T: (Lopicollo, forthcoming)
>
> R: Lopiccollo, Samuel T. Forthcoming. The relationship of injury and absenteeism in produce terminals: A quantitative study. *Journal of Human Resources* 19.

- Unknown journals that might be confused with similar journals list the place or institution of publication in parentheses.

- Follow the guideline in the books section for listing editors, compilers, or translators in addition to authors.

> B: Crown, Charles T., ed. "The Influence of Lighting Levels on Consumption of Alcohol in Drinking Establishments." *Advanced Graduate Research Journal* (Central Michigan University Mt. Pleasant) 3 (2007): 23–34.

Scientific Articles from a Database

- *Entries include the following* (if available):
  Database name
  URL
  Descriptive phrase or locator – for example an accession number or data marker
  Access date

Periodicals

> N: 1. Pathogen Database, http://www.foodpath. db.edu (accession number FP0228564; accessed May 31, 2008).

Journal and News Articles from a Database

- Follow the guidelines for printed periodicals.

- In addition to the full facts of publication, list the URL (after the publisher).

- Retrieval or access dates of Internet sites are typically not listed. Exceptions include time-sensitive fields such as law or medicine where small updates or corrections might be important (list after the URL).

> N: 2. Michelle Fraga, "Paradise is Owning a Lawn and Garden Shop," *Macomb Daily*, July 22, 2008, second edition, http://www.mdn.homeandgarden/com/.

Electronic Journals

- Follow the guidelines for printed journals.

- In addition, list the URL (after the publisher).

- List page numbers (if available).
- If page numbers are not available, add a descriptive locator (such as *under Work Related Stress* in the example below).

N: 4. Kevin W. LaPreis, "Situational Factors in Divorce," *Marriage and Counseling* 23 (2007), under "Work Related Stress," http://www.journal. uncc.edu/ mac/family/issues/t21/05924/05924.html.

- Retrieval or access dates of Internet sites are typically not listed. Exceptions include time-sensitive fields such as law or medicine where small updates or corrections might be important (list after the URL).

B: Simpson, Tamaqua R. "Advanced Surgery Techniques for Closed Head Injury." *Journal of Modern Medicine* 22, no. 4 (Summer 2007): 221–29. http://www.lcu.edu/pubs/surg/html.7732 (accessed October 12, 2007).

Periodicals

Magazines

- Follow many of the basic guidelines for journals.
- Cite by date (day, month, and year if available) even if issues or volumes are listed.
- Footnotes and endnotes list specific page numbers if referring to a specific passage. However, ranges of pages (such as 31–87) are typically avoided in bibliographies and reference lists since they are often widely separated by advertisements and other extraneous information.

N: 1. Cheryl Lapensee, "Benefits of Teacher Job Sharing in Public Schools," *Education*, April 13, 2008, 37.
B: Lapensee, Cheryl. "Benefits of Teacher Job Sharing in Public Schools." *Education*, April 13, 2008.
T: (Lapensee 2008)
R: Lapensee, Cheryl. 2008. Benefits of teacher job sharing in public schools. *Education*, April 13.

- Departments within magazines are capitalized headline style (without quotation marks).

N:	2. Ronald Meldrum, Alternative Musical Selections, *Hourly New Yorker*, December 1, 2008.
B:	Meldrum, Ronald. Alternative Musical Selections. *Hourly New Yorker*, December 1, 2008.

- Departments without authors are capitalized headline style (without quotation marks) and listed by magazine.

T:	(*Food Processing* 2007)
R:	*Food Processing.* 2007. Food for Thought. May.

Online Magazines

Periodicals

- Follow the guidelines for printed magazines.
- In addition, list the URL (after the date).

N:	3. Nicholas Ryan, "Potato Salad Extravaganza," *Food Preparation*, July 22, 2008, http://www.foodprep.com/salad/proc/issue/t33/83232.html.

- Retrieval or access dates of Internet sites are typically not listed. Exceptions include time-sensitive fields such as law or medicine where small updates or corrections might be important (list after the URL).

B:	Morell, Patrick. "Small Musical Instrument Repair is Big Business." *Business Design*, May 19, 2007. http://www.busdesign.com/article/music/4225.html.

- Page numbers are rarely available, but they are listed if found.
- Descriptive locators are not necessary for article length journals.

Newspapers

- Follow the basic guidelines for magazines.
- Omit *The* from the beginning of newspaper titles.

- Add cities even if the city is not part of the name (unless it is a well-known national paper).

- Add states (abbreviated) to unfamiliar cities.

- Add provinces (abbreviated) to unfamiliar Canadian cities.

- Add the cities (in parentheses) after names to foreign cities other than Canada.

The Boston Globe	should be	*Boston Globe*
The Gazette (from Baltimore, MD)	should be	*Baltimore Gazette*
The Wall Street Journal	should be	*Wall Street Journal*
The Bagley Press (from Bagley, Iowa)	should be	*Bagley (IA) Press*
Amory Times (from Amory, Mississippi)	should be	*Amory (MS) Times*
Herald (from London, England)	should be	*Herald (London)*

Periodicals

- Page numbers are typically omitted due to the potential number of editions that might be published in one day.

- Editions, section numbers, or other identifiers are listed (if available).

- Article titles in bibliographies, footnotes, and endnotes are capitalized headline style, and article titles in reference lists are capitalized sentence style. Convert article titles in full capital letters to uppercase and lowercase letters.

N:	1. Raymond Shearer, "Retail Sales Rebound on Strong December," *Detroit News,* May 31, 2008, late edition, sec. 1.
B:	Shearer, Raymond. "Retail Sales Rebound on Strong December." *Detroit News,* May 31, 2008, late edition, sec. 1.

> T: (Shearer 2008)
>
> R: Shearer, Raymond. 2008. Retail sales rebound on strong December. *Detroit News,* May 31, late edition, sec. 1.

Note: Newspapers citations are unique in one way. If all information is given in footnotes or endnotes, then corresponding entries are not necessary in bibliographies or reference lists (this is not required, but it is an option).

- Unsigned articles list the newspaper first.

> N: 2. *Montgomery (AL) Times*, "Red Cross responds to Hurricane Victims," June 12, 2007.

- *Letters to the editor* are treated generically with no headline.

Periodicals

> N: 3. Shonnell Wonders, letter to the editor, *Boston Globe,* December 17, 2008.

- News service names are capitalized, but not italicized.

> N: 4. Associated Press, "America's Gambling Addiction," *New York Times*, January 22, 2008.

Online Newspapers

- Follow the guidelines for printed newspapers.
- In addition, list the URL (after the date).
- Retrieval or access dates of Internet sites are typically not listed. Exceptions include time-sensitive fields such as law or medicine where small updates or corrections might be important (list after the URL).
- Page numbers are rarely available, but they are listed if found.
- Descriptive locators are not necessary.

> B: Stankovich, Shannon. "Chicago Teens Gain Respect as Debaters." *Cincinnati Gazette,* March 15, 2008. http://www.cingaz.com/2008/march/youth/issues/t31/94436.html.

Reviews (of books, movies, plays, television shows, concerts, etc.)

List Entries in the Following Order:
  Reviewer(s)
  Review title – if available
  Work being reviewed
  Author(s), editor(s), directors, or *translators(s)* of work
      being reviewed
  Location – if a performance
  Date of review – if a performance
  URL – for Internet or other electronic sources
  Periodical – where the review appears
  Periodical publication information – if available

Book

N:	1. Janelle Summers, "New Perspectives in Focus Group Research," review of *Focus Groups: Reinventing the Wheel,* by Helen P. Davis, *Journal of Social Commentary* 10 (May 2008): 212–27.

Play

N:	1. Whitford, Bradley, review of *Past Days of Glory,* by Stephen Tyler, directed by Joseph Perry, Hamilton-Kramer Theater, Boston, *Boston Times,* September 4, 2008, early edition.

- Unsigned reviews follow the guidelines for unsigned newspaper articles.

Interviews

- Best cited in footnotes or endnotes (rarely in bibliographies or reference lists)

List Entries in the Following Order:
  Person being interviewed
  Interviewer
  Identifying information – if available
  Place of interview – if available
  Date of interview
  Accessibility – if available

Unpublished Interviews

> N: 1. James Plecas, interview by Kathleen Junge about the growth of Idaho high school basketball, Des Moines, May 21, 2008, tape recording, Idaho Sports Collection, Ashton, ID.

Unattributed Interviews (people who prefer to remain anonymous)
- The absence of a name needs to be explained in text (i.e. the interviewed person's name was withheld so current and future narcotics investigations would not be hindered).

> N: 2. Interview with undercover narcotics officer, March 14, 2007.

Published Interviews

> N: 3. Rafael Crickles, interview by Reginald Chude, *Speaking Out*, CBS, February 4, 2008.

Personal Communication

- Best cited in footnotes or endnotes (rarely in bibliographies or reference lists)

Email
- Specific email addresses are not listed unless permission is obtained from the owner.

> N: 1. Alonzo R. King, email message to Ed
> Schneider, June 21, 2008.

Telephone

- Specific telephone numbers are not listed unless permission is obtained from the owner.

Personal Communication

> N: 2. Katie Pakreetious, telephone conversation with the author, September 29, 2007.

Face-to-Face

> N: 3. Suellen Janesworth, personal communication with the author, January 26, 2008.

Unpublished Works

In General

- Material posted on the Internet is technically considered published. However, follow the guidelines for unpublished works when citing most posted Internet material.

- Titles are not italicized.

- Titles are capitalized headline style in quotation marks for footnotes, endnotes, and bibliographies. Titles are capitalized sentence style without quotation marks for reference lists.

Unpublished Works

> N: 1. Louis C. Rouhib, "Techniques for Snow Removal Equipment Repair" (computer printout, Department of Mechanical Engineering, Western Montana University, 2008).
>
> R: Rouhib, Louis C. 2008. Techniques for snow removal equipment repair. Computer printout, Department of Mechanical Engineering, Western Montana Univ.

Dissertations and Theses

> N: 2. Dale M. Plotkowski, "The Influence of Verbal
> Aggressiveness on Maintenance Personnel in a
> Manufacturing Environment" (master's thesis,
> Indiana State University, 2007), 132–34.
>
> B: Plotkowski, Dale M. "The Influence of Verbal
> Aggressiveness on Maintenance Personnel in a
> Manufacturing Environment." Master's thesis,
> Indiana State University, 2007.

Lectures or Papers Presented at Meetings

- List the title followed by the sponsor (organization, as-sociation, etc.), location (where the speech was given or paper was presented), and date.

Unpublished Works

> B: Franklin, Patricia R. "Black Catholics in The United
> States." Paper presented at the annual meeting of
> the Council for Diversity and Religion, Dallas,
> TX, March 7-9, 2008.

Patents

- Cite under creator name(s) and year of filing.
- Include patent number (if available).

> R: Eschner, Eva, and Roy Bryant. 2006. Exhaust noise
> reduction system. US Patent 5,495,336, filed Oct.
> 15, 2006, and issued Feb. 6, 2008.

Manuscripts

- List the title, date of item (list range if necessary), series title (if applicable), name of collection, and name and location of depository.
- For more detailed guidelines, follow *The Guide to the National Archives of the United States* (use an Internet search engine to find *The Guide to the National Archives of the United States*).

N:	3. Edward Cendrowski's Polish War Memoirs, 18 May 1944, World War II Series, Warsaw Collection of Polish Manuscripts, Philadelphia Historical Archives, Pennsylvania.
B:	Polish Manuscripts. Warsaw Collection. Philadelphia Historical Archives, Pennsylvania.
N:	4. Minutes of the Committee for Ending Slavery, 1860-1864, Papers of the New England Society for Slavery Abolition, Massachusetts Historical Archives, Boston.
B:	England Society for Slavery Abolition. Papers. Massachusetts Historical Archives, Boston.

Electronic Mailing Lists
- List author (if available), name of list, date of posting, and URL (if the list is archived online).
- Retrieval or access dates of Internet sites are typically not listed. Exceptions include time-sensitive fields such as law or medicine where small updates or corrections might be important (list after the URL).

Unpublished Works

N:	5. Stanley Tomczyk, e-mail to Celiac mailing list, August 17, 2008, http://www.healthchanges.net/celiac/concerns/87334.html (accessed December 8, 2008).

Personal Websites
- Best cited in footnotes or endnotes (if used).
- List content author, title of site (in quotation marks), owner of site, and URL.
- Retrieval or access dates of Internet sites are typically not listed. Exceptions include time-sensitive fields such as law or medicine where small updates or corrections might be important (list after the URL).

N:	7. William Whidden's official Web site, "Musical Influences," Yolanda Whidden, http://www.williamwhidden.com/music/chat/88.html.

- List author (if available), title of site (in quotation marks), owner of site, and URL.

- Retrieval or access dates of Internet sites are typically not listed. Exceptions include time-sensitive fields such as law or medicine where small updates or corrections might be important (list after the URL).

Unpublished Works

N:	6. Chattanooga Public Library Chief Financial Officer, "Chattanooga Public Library 2007 Profit and Loss Statement," Chattanooga Public Library, http://www.chatpublib.org/cfo/pandl/plan/99834.html.

Special References

Dictionaries and Encyclopedias

- Reference books that are well-known are generally cited in notes rather than bibliographies. Publication facts are not necessary, although the edition is required.

Special References

- List the title (italicized), edition (not volume and page numbers), and item (proceeded by s.v. [sub verbo]).

N:	1. *Encyclopedia Britannica*, 14th ed., s.v. "Hemispheres."
N:	2. *Dictionary of Modern Marvels*, 4th ed., s.v. "Airplanes."

Other Works

- List all publication details.

N:	3. *MLA Handbook for Writers of Research Papers*, 6th ed., Joseph Gibaldi (New York: Modern Language Association of America), 5.4.

Online Dictionaries and Encyclopedias

- Follow printed guidelines, but list URL and access dates.

N:	4. *Encyclopedia Britannica Online*, s.v. "Beauty Pageants," http://search.eb.com/ bio/birds/ subjecttj5933.sci (accessed February 15, 2007).

Brochures, Pamphlets, and Reports

- List like books.

N:	5. Raymond V. Roiek, *Migratory Game Birds* (Warren, MI: Warren Tackle and Bait Shop, 2008).

Microform

- List like books, but also give page number (of printed text), fiche, frame, and row (if available).

N:	6. Jean Wojtaszak, *Packaging Mythology in Forming Film* (Miami: University of Miami Press, 2007), text-fiche, p. 67, 5D14.

Abstract

- List like journals, but add the word *abstract.*

B:	Rutherford, Lori A. "New Technology in Heart Transplant Surgery" (Valve Formation, France). Abstract. *American Journal of Medicine* 31 (2005): 264.

Special References

Scriptural References

Christian or Jewish Scriptures

- List book (abbreviated), chapter, and verse (no page number).

For a chapter and verse in Luke (The New Testament)	
N:	1. Lk. 12:3–21.
T:	(Lk. 12:3–21)
For a chapter and verse in Amos (Jewish Bible/The Old Testament)	
N:	2. Am. 4:12.
T:	(Am. 4:12)

Scriptural References

Versions of the Bible

Scriptural References

- Work intended for general readers lists the version (at least on the first reference).

> *For a chapter and verse in James (The New Testament) from the New Revised Standard Version*
>
> N: 3. Jas. 4:13–16 (New Revised Standard Version).

Other Sacred Texts (i.e. Qur'an, Upanishads)

- Follow basic guidelines for other Christian or Jewish scriptures.

- More authoritative guidelines are found in the *History of Religions Journal* (use an Internet search engine to find *History of Religions Journal*)

Classical English Plays and Poems

Classical English Plays and Poems

- Typically list book, canto, and stanza.

> N: 1. Chaucer, "The Clerk's Prologue," *Canterbury Tales*, fragment 4, lines 7–49.

Musical Scores

Published Scores

- Follow basic guidelines for books.

Musical Scores

> R: Mozart, Wolfgang Amadeus. 1956. *Sonatas and fantasies for the piano*. Prepared from the autographs and earliest printed sources by Jerry Pokorny. Rev. ed. Fryeburg, ME: Landsford.

Audiovisual Materials

Entries Include the Following (if available):
  Composer, writer, performer, or other primary person
  Title
  Recording company or publisher
  Recording identification number
  Medium – CD, audiocassette, etc.
  Copyright date, production date, URL, or other information
    – might also be listed if helpful

Discographies

- List under a separate page titled *Discography*.

- For example, assume Robert Bigger is a Jazz musician (list titles in chronological order starting with the oldest).

---

1. Listing by Artist and Composition Titles

BIGGER, ROBERT

"Walkin' Home," March 13, 1963. *My Life,* Blue Note
  BST-67396.

"Night in Harlem," January 14, 1964. *Holding a Hard Line,*
  Blue Note BST-69665.

"Living in Your World," May 12, 1966. *Liar's Breath,* Blue
  Note BST-74503.

Musical Recordings

- Use for other than discographies.

N: 1. Robert Stinson, *Moonlight Blues*, Charity Records,
         Dolby HX TRC, Audiocassette.

Lectures or Readings (recordings of drama, prose, or poetry)

N: 2. Timothy Domanski, *Principles of Chemical Engineering*, audiotapes of lectures by Steven Hanisits and Edward Barth at the meeting of the Society for Chemical Engineers, Baltimore, January 14, 2007 (New Orleans: University of New Orleans Press, 2008).

N: 3. Doreen Kadjan, *Silver Wings,* performed by Peter Lambert and Scott Chandonette, Carriage Valley Records, CDLS-2007 (compact disc).

CD-ROMs or DVD-ROMs

- List the same as printed works.
- Publication place and date are omitted (unless relevant).

Audiovisual Materials

B: *American Standard Dictionary.* 4th ed. CD-ROM, version 3.0. Louisiana State University Press.

B: *Complete Rolling Stone Magazine.* CD-ROM. Envision, 2008.

Filmstrips and Slides

N: 4. Bradley Jacokes, *Gardens of Southern Michigan* (Williamston, MI: Gardener Education, 2008), slides.

Videos and DVDs

- List scenes (in DVD) following the guidelines for chapters in books.

N: 5. Angelina Boscarino, "Symbolic Spanish Gestures," *Cultural Meanings*, DVD, directed by Carlo Bautista (Santa Monica, CA: Sylvan Home Entertainment, 2008).

Legal Citations

In General

- Three different guides are acceptable for use, but for simplification purposes, *The ALWD Citation Manual: A Professional System of Citation* will be used for this book. For more in-depth detail on these guidelines, use an Internet search engine to find and order *The ALWD Citation Manual: A Professional System of Citation.*

- Italicize case names, titles of articles, titles of chapters, uncommon non-English words or phrases, and words indicating emphasis.

- Omit periods from abbreviations of names that are explained or recognizable. However, some abbreviations require periods.

- Most legal works use notes only.

N:	1. *NAACP v. Chicago Packing Co.*, 207 F.4e 361 n. 2 (9th Cir. 2008).

- Below are some examples of abbreviations that require periods.

v.	*is used for*	versus
n.	*is used for*	note
F.	*is used for*	Federal Reporter
F. Supp.	*is used for*	Federal Supplement
U.S.	*is used for*	United States Supreme Court Reporter
ch.	*is used for*	chapter
Cir	*is used for*	Circuit
ed.	*is used for*	editor or edition

Books or Treatises

- Capitalize titles headline style.
- Use & instead of *and* to separate authors.

> N: 2. Lakisha Johnson & James Victor Crawford,
>   *Federal Grants Laws for Small Business* ch. 10 (4th
>   ed., Sims Press 2007).

Chapters in Edited Books

- List the title of the chapter and the book (both are italicized).
- List the first page of the chapter and the specific page cited.

> N: 3. Mary McBride, *Freedom of Information Act,* in
>   *Law and Pubic Access* 112, 117 (Michael Molnar
>   ed., Rupkis 2008).

Legal Citations

Articles in Periodicals

- Well-known journals are abbreviated. Article titles are italicized.
- List volume numbers in arabic (before the journal name)
- List the first page of the chapter and the specific page cited (after the journal name).
- List the date last (in parentheses)

> N: 4. Stephen Frishman, *Verbal Aggression in The*
>   Courtroom, 174 Yale L. J. 1263, 1275 (2007).

Court Decisions or Cases

- *Entries include the following* (if available):
  Case names
  Volume number – in arabic
  Reporter series – abbreviated
  Ordinal series number – if applicable
  Abbreviated name of court and date – in parentheses
- List the opening page of the decision and the specific page cited.

> N: 5. *Joann Dahms v. Cupples Manufacturing*, 314
>   F.4d 245, 253 (7th Cir. 2008).

United States Supreme Court Decisions
- Published cases cite to *United States Supreme Court Reporter*. Not yet published cases cite to the *Supreme Court Reporter*.

> N: 6. *Swift Provision v. USDA FSIS*, 621 U.S. 223 (2007).

Lower Federal Court Decisions
- Cite to the *Federal Reporter* or the *Federal Supplement*.

> N: 7. *Milton Vogel v. EPA*, 191 F. 304 (4th Cir. 2006).

State and Local Court Decisions
- Cite to the official state reporter.

> N: 8. *Schreck v. Corrigan*, 92 Cal. 2d 856 (2007).

Constitutions
- List article, amendment numbers, and other subdivision numbers.

> N: 9. U.S. Const. art. VI, §2.

Public Documents

In General
- *Entries include the following* (if available):
  Country, state, county, city, or other government entity issuing the document
  Executive department, legislative body, board, court bureau, committee, or commission
  Regional offices, subsidiary divisions, or similar
  Document or collection title – if available
  Author, editor, compiler, or translator – if available
  Report number – or other identifying information
  Publisher – if different from issuing body
  Date
  Page – if available

- Identify congress and session.

N: 1. Senate Committee on Illegal Immigration, *The Immigration Act of 2008*, 114th Cong., 2d sess., 2008, S. Rep. 3246, 10–13.

B: U.S. Congress. Senate. Committee on Illegal Immigration. *The Immigration Act of 2008*. 114th Cong., 2d sess., 2008. S. Rep. 3246.

T: (U.S. Senate Committee 2008,10–13*)*

R: U.S. Congress. Senate. Committee on Illegal Immigration. 2008. *The Immigration Act of 2008*. 114th Cong., 2d sess. S. Rep. 3246.

- Use 3-em dash for repeated references to the same congressional source.

Public Documents

B: U.S. Congress. Senate. Committee on Global Warming. *Water Regulation...*

————. Committee on Global Warming. *Earth Changes...*

————. Committee on Global Warming. *Air Quality and...*

Documents and Reports

- Use *H.* For House and *S.* for Senate references.
- List Congress number, session number, and series number (if available).

B: U.S. Congress. House. *Report on Food Security in USDA Inspected Poultry Slaughtering Facilities*. 110th Cong., 1st sess., 2007. H. Doc. 499.

Hearings (records of testimony before congressional committees)
- List titles

B: U.S. Congress. Senate. Committee on Endangered Species. *Wolves in the Southwestern United States: Hearing before the Committee on Endangered Species*. 112th Cong., 1st sess., March 23, 2008.

Resolutions and Bills
- Use *HR* for House of Representatives and *S* for Senate references.
- List title of bill (italicized), bill number, congressional session, and congressional record publication details (if available).

N:	2. *Bank Reserve Act of 2006*, HR 2450, 101st Cong., 2d sess., *Congressional Record 212*, no. 154, daily ed. (November 25, 2006): H 8732.

Statutes and Public Laws
- Cite as statutes.

N:	3. *Health and Welfare Reform Act of 2008*, Public Law 714–717, *U.S. Statutes at Large* 123 (2008): 71.

Municipal Ordinances and State Laws
- List the ordinance or law, the code, and the year the volume was supplemented or updated (along with a name, if available, to indicate the version of the code).

N:	4. *Iowa Rev. Code Ann* § 4129.34 (Winters 2007).

Executive Department Documents
- Includes reports, circulars, and bulletins issued by bureaus and agencies.
- List authors (if available).

N:	5. Darnell T. Anderson, *Mutual Fund Investment for Upper and Middle Class Americans*, special report prepared at the request of the Department of Finance, March 2008, 27–29.

Census Bureau
- List bureau, title, and preparing division.

N:	6. U.S. Bureau of the Census. *Median Household Income by State in the United States, 2008*. Prepared by the Housing Division, Bureau of the Census. Washington, DC, 2008.

Public Documents

Government Commissions

- Includes reports, circulars, and studies issued by commissions such as the SEC or FCC.

- List commission and title.

> B: U.S. Federal Communications Commission. *Annual Report of the Federal Communications Commission for the Fiscal Year.* Washington, DC: GPO, 2007.

Constitutions (Federal or State)

- List constitution, article or amendment, section, and clause (if applicable)

> N: 7. U.S. Constitution, art. 3, sec. 2, cl. 3.
>
> N: 8. U.S. Constitution, amend. 13, sec. 3.
>
> N: 9. Wyoming Constitution, art. 5, sec. 1.

Public Documents

State and Local Governments

- Follow guidelines for federal governments

> N.   10. Kentucky General Assembly, Tax Assessment Commission, *Report to the 95th General Assembly of the State of Kentucky* (Louisville, 2007), 12–17.

International Bodies

- Examples of acceptable abbreviations are listed below.

OPEC	*is used for*	Organization of Petroleum Exporting Countries
UN	*is used for*	United Nations
WTO	*is used for*	World Trade Organization
GATT	*is used for*	General Agreement on Tariffs and Trade

- List authorizing body (and author or editor if applicable), topic or title, date, series (if available), publication information (if available), and pages (if available).

N: 11. L. C. Johnson, "Chinese Trade Barriers to Western Countries," in *International Trade and Economy*, ed. B. Larson, chap. 6, Discussion Paper 174 (Geneva: WTO, 2007).

Online Public Documents

- Follow guidelines for printed documents.

- In addition to the full facts of publication, list the URL (after the publisher).

- Retrieval or access dates of Internet sites are typically not listed. Exceptions include time-sensitive fields such as law or medicine where small updates or corrections might be important (list after the URL).

Public Documents

N: 12. Michigan Constitution, art. 1, sec. 3, http:// www.ligis.state.mi.us/ constitution/libry/terran24. html (accessed June 14, 2008).

B: Michigan Constitution, art. 1, sec. 3. http://www. ligis.state.mi.us/constitution/libry/ terran24.html (accessed June 14, 2008).

T: (Michigan Constitution)

R: Michigan Constitution, art. 1, sec. 3. http://www. ligis.state.mi.us/constitution/libry/ terran24.html (accessed June 14, 2008).

Part Four
Sample Paper

Paper Setup

In General

- Use 8.5 x 11 inch paper (non-erasable type).

- Print on one side of the paper only.

- Use an easily readable font (i.e. 12 point Times New Roman).

- The title is single spaced and centered in uppercase letters in the top third of the title page. If there is a subtitle, place a colon after the title and center the subtitle in uppercase letters on the following line (continue single spacing).

- The author's name, course, date, and any other information required by the instructor are centered in upper and lowercase letters several lines below the title on the title page. Each piece of information is placed on a separate line with single spacing between.

- Do not number the title page.

- Margins are one inch on all sides for the text, notes, bibliography, and references.

- Use left justification only (no right or full justification) for the text, notes, bibliographies, and reference lists.

- Double-space the entire text portion of the document (with the exception of long quotations).

- Single space individual footnote and endnote entries with a double space between each entry.

- For footnote and endnote entries, indent the first line 3 spaces and leave the following lines flush with the left margin.

- Single space individual biography and reference list entries with a double space between each entry.

- For bibliography and reference list entries, make the first line flush with the left margin and indent the following lines 3 spaces.

- Use one space (not two) after periods at the end of sentences and after colons.

- Number pages consecutively with arabic numerals starting at the first page of text. The page number on the first page of text is 2. The arabic numerals are listed flush right in the header.

- Indent paragraphs five spaces (using the tab key).

- Turn off the automatic hyphenation function.

- Avoid underlining throughout the document.

- Indent long quotations (three or more lines of poetry or two or more sentences of prose) five spaces (using the tab key) using single spacing. Quotation marks are not used for long quotations.

Note: The following sample paper is geared toward students in academia, and the *Chicago Manual of Style* does not contain such a paper. However, academic writing is discussed in Kate Turabian's *A Manual for Writers of Term Papers, Theses, and Dissertations* (7th Edition).

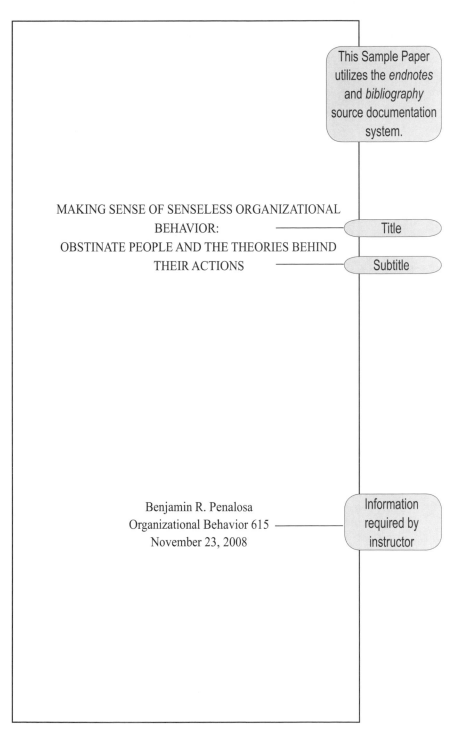

This Sample Paper utilizes the *endnotes* and *bibliography* source documentation system.

MAKING SENSE OF SENSELESS ORGANIZATIONAL BEHAVIOR:

— Title

OBSTINATE PEOPLE AND THE THEORIES BEHIND THEIR ACTIONS

— Subtitle

Benjamin R. Penalosa
Organizational Behavior 615
November 23, 2008

Information required by instructor

Background

Obstinate employees in organizations can be defined as individuals who hinder, rather than help, other people get their jobs done. These people are not necessarily unlikable, nor do they always have bad ideas; they just tend to make others' jobs harder. Diane Malicki makes the following observation:

> There is no blueprint for a successful organization.
> Some succeed with great product lines or marketing
> strategies, others by hard work, and still others rely
> on factors such as luck or being in the right place at
> the right time. However, academic research indicates
> that most successful organizations have one thing in
> common...they designate goals for employees. Successful
> organizations believe that goals are very important, and
> goal achievement is absolutely essential for organizational
> survival. However, sometimes people who want to
> accomplish things are hindered by those who do not.
> The negative behavior of these hindering individuals can
> produce a rippling effect throughout an organization, and
> that is precisely why it needs to be stopped.[1]

Obstinate employees have been the focus of recent research due to their impact on others within the organization. Joseph Dubose found them to negatively influence coworkers, thereby impeding organizational efficiency and productivity.[2]

Obstinate people include talkers and opinionaters. These individuals are described, exemplified, and theoretically explained.

Talkers

Talkers are people who "tell other employees how much work they have to do . . . but that is the extent of their actions."[3] These employees normally do not take a lot of time off work and understand what needs to be done for the organization to operate efficiently. They make a point, however, of telling any person who will listen about their work related concerns. The listener is forced to hear day after day about the talker's problems. Many people come to the conclusion that if the talker would quit complaining and do his or her job, many of these "problems" would disappear. Carlita Miguel termed these employees "visible in attendance, yet invisible in production."[4]

A custodian from an insurance office fit the talker mode quite well. This individual worked the day shift in the office, performing various janitorial duties. However, he often fell behind in his work or did not complete it because spent a good portion of time complaining to other employees. He continually talked about the low wage he received for the massive amount of work that he needed to get done.

At first, employees were empathetic and let the janitor finish talking. However, after he repeated the same basic troubles over and over, people began to either avoid him or question why he was not doing his job instead of talking about it. When coworkers challenged his work ethic he got upset and often ended up arguing with his accusers.

The janitor was written up by management several times for getting into conflicts with other employees. He did not change his ways, was never promoted, and continued airing his problems…with the only difference being that he no longer had people who would listen to him.

Adam's Equity Theory explains the janitor's actions.[5] This theory involves employees who compare their inputs and results to that of other employees and feel some type of inequity. In this case, the janitor believed he was doing lot of work and not being properly compensated for it. He became bitter about the situation and decided to spend his time complaining to others instead of performing his job functions. His response to the perceived "inequity" was a decrease in personal workload and a negative attitude. He attempted to eliminate the inequity, but in reality his actions did little to resolve the problem.

Opinionaters

Opinionaters are individuals focused on their own viewpoints. They generally believe everything they say is a fact and everything they do is the best way. If others disagree with them, they usually argue their point until their opponent gives up or walks away.[6]

Opinionaters are often the most difficult people to deal with because they are normally quite knowledgeable and often speak the truth, regardless of who is offended or embarrassed. They frequently voice their beliefs in front of an audience because they have a lot of faith in themselves.

Opinionaters generally do not fear arguing race, religion, or politics. They can swing from one side of the religious or political spectrum to the other as they progress through different stages of life. In youth they may have liberal perspectives, but aging tends to bring on more conservative viewpoints. These shifts are often the result of changes in financial status.[7]

One opinionater in a 10-store grocery chain was quite knowledgeable of the overall operation. She had grown up in the business and eventually ran it when the founders, her father and his two brothers, decided to retire.

She was very open about arguing her strong Republican Party affiliation. Since politics is a sensitive matter to some people, her opinions got her in trouble with a variety of employees, suppliers, and customers.

Paraphrasing from a journal

Paraphrasing from a newspaper

Her points were fairly well researched and valid, but she never considered the fact that she might be creating tension and enemies. She was more interested in establishing her viewpoint than she was in growing her business. Sometimes her adversaries simply laughed or remained silent while she argued her position, but other times they refuted her ideas. If a democratic viewpoint was expressed, a rebuttal was sure to follow and this debate had the potential of escalating into a heated argument with verbal assaults.

Some individuals commented that this woman never thought she was wrong and there's no discussion. This left them feeling bitter toward the grocery store chain because they saw the opinionater as personifying the organization, and her actions were construed as those of the company.

Eventually, the chain of grocery stores had to be sold due to declining sales. The opinionater received enough money to modestly retire on, but many people felt she would have done much better if she had not alienated so many people with her strong viewpoints.

The Opinionater's action can be explained by The Cyclical Theory of Opinion and Self-Perception.[8] This theory proposes people analyze issues and choose to form opinions or decline to form opinions in order to establish self-perception.

People who form opinions associate with individuals of the same opinion and disassociate with those of differing opinion. Regardless of the association or disassociation, people who form opinions establish a perception of how they would like others to view them. They have taken positions that help define themselves. This self-perception is reinforced when these individuals analyze other issues and make similar opinion related decisions.

People who do not form opinions do not associate or disassociate with others who have developed opinions. This abstinence from association or disassociation helps these individuals establish a desired perception of themselves. They avoid the conflict (functional or non-functional) that can result from associating or disassociating with others and take a position of middle of the road or non-confrontational. The self-perception generated from the choice to remain neutral is reinforced when these individuals choose a similar opinion pathway when confronted with different issues.

The opinionater in the 10-store grocery chain wanted to be viewed as an authority whose opinions should not be challenged. She was not afraid of disassociating herself with others, regardless of the potential harm that might be inflicted upon her business. She focused on position…and reinforced that position with her opinion on a variety of political issues.

Conclusion

Many organizations have experienced at least one of the two types of obstinate employees discussed in this paper. Working with obstinate people in business can be challenging, but it is possible if a person realizes what he or he is up against.[9]

Please note that some of the information for this paper stemmed from the work of psychologist Robert M. Bramson, who discussed individuals who hinder others' job performances in detail.[10]

7

Notes — Endnotes are placed after the text on a separate page

1. Diane L. Malicki, "Obstinate Employee Behavior in Organizations," *Journal of Organizational Behavior* 21 (2008): 149.

(Journal with one author)
(Page number of quote)

2. Joseph Dubose, "Employee Parachutes," in *Organizational Blame: Excuses and Explanations* (Troy, MI: Avonhurst Books, 2007), 207–23.

3. Jadwiga Berisha and Maryanne Sunda, *Employee Actions and Consequences* (Sedona, AZ: Fradello Books, 2007): 127.

4. Carlita A. Miguel, "Difficult Employee Behavior," *Organizational Review* 22, no.5 (Summer 2007): 217. http://www.oru.edu/pub/syst/html.7819.

(Online journal with no access date because it is not time sensitive)

5. J. Stacy Adams, "Inequity in Social Exchange," in *Advances in Experimental Social Psychology*, ed. by Leonard Berkowicz (New York: Academic Press, 1965), 267–300.

(Book with editor, first initial and middle name)

6. Julia F. Schaffer, "Opinions and Beliefs: A Quantitative Analysis," *Journal of Social Commentary* 23 (2007): 212.

7. *Wall Street Journal*, "Political Viewpoints and Aging," May 14, 2008.

(Newspaper title – No author)

8. Timothy J. Houghton and Peggy M. Houghton, *Theories of Self-Presentation* (Flint, MI: Baker College, forthcoming).

(Book with two authors, forthcoming)

9. Malicki, "Obstinate Employee Behavior," 151.

(Shortened subsequent note citation)

10. R. M. Bramson, *Coping with Difficult People* (New York: Doubleday, 1981).

(Book with one author, initials only)

Bibliography is placed after the endnotes on a separate page	Bibliography

Adams, J. Stacy. "Inequity in Social Exchange." In *Advances in Experimental Social Psychology*. Edited by Leonard Berkowicz. New York: Academic Press, 1965.

Berisha, Jadwiga, and Maryanne Sunda. *Employee Actions and Consequences*. Sedona, AZ: Fradello Books, 2007.

Bramson, R. M. *Coping with Difficult People*. New York: Doubleday, 1981.

Chapter in a book

Dubose, Joseph. "Employee Parachutes." Chap. 8 in *Organizational Blame: Excuses and Explanations*. Troy, MI: Avonhurst Books, 2007.

Houghton, Timothy J., and Peggy M. Houghton. *Theories of Self-Presentation*. Flint, MI: Baker College, forthcoming.

Malicki, Diane L. "Obstinate Employee Behavior in Organizations." *Journal of Organizational Behavior* 21 (2008): 147–153.

Miguel, Carlita A. "Difficult Employee Behavior." *Organizational Review* 22, no.5 (Summer 2007): 211–23. http://www.oru.edu/pub/syst/html.7819.

Schaffer, Julia F. "Opinions and Beliefs: A Quantitative Analysis." *Journal of Social Commentary* 23 (2007): 204–217.

Unsigned newspaper article

Wall Street Journal. "Political Viewpoints and Aging." May 14, 2008

Index

H

Hanging indents 2, 4
Hearings 82
Historical events 7
Holidays 7

I

Ibid 20, 41
Illustrations 21-24
Institutions 6
International bodies 84
Interviews 70
Introductions 57

J

Journals 60-63, 92, 95
Judicial divisions 15

L

Lectures 72, 78
Legal citations 79, 80
Line spacing 1, 3

M

Magazines 60, 65
Manuscripts 72
Margins 1, 3
Mathematical expressions 28, 29
Microform 75
Military terms 8
Military titles 31
Military units 14
Months 7
Movies 9
Multiple authors 44
Multi volumes 58
Municipal ordinances 83
Musical recordings 77
Musical scores 76
Musical works 10

N

Names of organizations 6
Newspapers 60, 66-68, 92, 95, 96
Notes and bibliography system 35
Numbers 11, 12, 15

O

Online dictionaries 74
Online encyclopedias 74
Online journals 95
Online magazines 66
Online newspapers 68
Online public documents 85
Online sources 10, 74
Operas 10
Organizations 32

P

Page numbering 2-4
Page setup 91
Paintings 11
Paper setup 87
Paragraph indentation 2, 4
Paraphrasing 92
Parenthetical citations 47
Patents 72
Percentages 13
Periodicals 8, 13, 60-68
Personal communication 70, 71
Personal names 5, 31
Personal websites 73
Physical quantities 12
Places of worship 15
Plagiarism 34
Plays 9
Poems 9
Prefaces 57
Publication facts 52, 54
Public documents 81-85
Public laws 83

Q

Quotations 16-21, 90
Quotation marks 18

R

Radio 9
Readings 78
Recordings 10
References 36, 43
Reference lists 48, 50
Resolutions 83

Also by Houghton & Houghton:

APA: THE EASY WAY!

For many writers, the most difficult part of writing a research paper is the mechanics of putting that paper together... the detailed specifications regarding spacing, capitalization, citing of sources, etc. Many researchers deplore this part of the project and long to simply blurt out research findings...without any regard for spelling, punctuation, grammar, or protocol.

This book simplifies the mechanics of communicating an idea or ideas to others in a scholarly fashion. The writer must abide by the rules and regulations governing the publication of research...so writers need to learn what the rules are and conform to them accordingly. Consequently, ideas will be properly explained, communicated, understood, and appreciated.

MLA: THE EASY WAY!

This book clarifies important aspects of Modern Language Association (MLA) guidelines by providing excellent supplemental support. Frequently used aspects of MLA style, citation, and referencing are addressed in a simple format that allows researchers to focus on content instead of mechanics and style.

The intent of this handbook is simply to supplement the official *MLA Handbook for Writers of Research Papers* (6th edition). It is provided as a condensed version of the actual manual. It is not intended to supersede the manual, rather reduce its complexity.

Quite simply, *MLA: The Easy Way!* presents the basics of MLA style in a clear, concise, accurate, and easy-to-navigate package. Try it, and immediately relieve some of the stress of writing a research paper.

Education is one of the best investments you will ever make...and our books maximize that investment!

Houghton & Houghton